Master Key Arcana

by

Charles F. Haanel
and others

Edited by Anthony R. Michalski

Kallisti Publishing
Wilkes-Barre, PA

Other books by Charles F. Haanel...

The Master Key System
The Amazing Secrets of the Yogi
A Book About You
The New Psychology
Mental Chemistry

Master Key Arcana by Charles F. Haanel

Published by
Kallisti Publishing, 332 Center Street, Wilkes-Barre, PA, 18702

FIRST EDITION

Other fine books published by Kallisti Publishing are available from your local bookstore or direct from the publisher.

Library of Congress Control Number: 2004109505

ISBN 0-9678514-4-0

Kallisti Publishing
332 Center Street, Wilkes-Barre, PA 18702
Phone (877) 444-6188 • Fax (419) 781-1907
www.kallistipublishing.com

This book is dedicated to...

My Mother and Father;
Mr. Haanel, that his teachings may continue to inspire;
Charlie: teacher, business man, friend;
all of the writers and teachers of great ideas and thoughts;
the American Free Enterprise System;
and God.

Master Key Arcana

Table of Contents

Master Key Arcana
Table of Contents

Introduction by Anthony R. Michalski

It is my pleasure to enclose herewith... Master Key Arcana. As Mr. Haanel so kindly began his historic tome, so I begin this collection of Haanel and Master Key-related documents.

Charles F. Haanel's writings, most notably The Master Key System, influenced me greatly, as they have influenced many others. Since first republishing The Master Key System in 2000, I have received emails and letters from folks living around the globe. Some have written that their parents had read it to them when they were children! It isn't uncommon for couples to read it to each other and discuss it. As a fellow from Australia wrote:

> "My wife and I have been reading aloud and discussing passages all morning quite forgetting our normal work. To say we read with delight tells only half the story as the book is also deeply challenging and one might even say awesome in it's implications."

I am highly confident that many of you already know how powerful The Master Key System is. If you are not, then you will be after you read it—especially after being "teased" by the contents of this book. But what exactly is this Master Key Arcana?, you are probably asking yourself.

Master Key Arcana is a collection of writings by Charles F. Haanel that were "lost" and have not been published in any form in over sixty years. Master Key Arcana also contains writings by other luminaries whom Mr. Haanel referenced in his classic work. It began when I obtained a version of The Master Key System that had twenty-eight parts in it. I had never seen that! The only version of which I knew was twenty-four parts, which I re-termed "Weeks" in Kallisti's publication of the book in order to facilitate easier reading and study. I researched and found nothing about these "missing" parts. When I obtained other works by Haanel, I checked to see if they were teaser chapters for other books, but alas that was not the case. They were indeed additional parts to Haanel's seminal work.

Thus, I decided to publish these "lost" parts and other items I found along the way as I researched Haanel and his works. The "lost" parts are excellent pieces and add even more depth to The Master Key System. They get a little more metaphysical–if that is possible!–and begin the journey to his later works, such as The New Psychology or A Book About You. I am certain that you will garner great insights as you read these parts.

The Master Key Psychological Chart came from a brochure that I assume Haanel used to market The Master Key System. It really is a powerful tool, though. Many people–the author most definitely included–sometimes wonder what standard to use when judging themselves as to where they stand in regard to their pursuit of excellence. This chart not only gives a grading system for self-evaluation, but it provides a list of the characteristics at which to look and evaluate. It is very illuminating to see where one stands presently in an objective and true way. I highly encourage you to work with this chart and to do the exercise as vigilantly and thoroughly as you would do any exercise in The Master Key System. Do as the philosopher Socrates stated: "Know thyself!"

In that same brochure were many letters of praise and thanks from readers and students of The Master Key System. I included Dr. Sanjivi's review in this little tome. Not only did Dr. Sanjivi's renown provoke me to include it, but also to add some concrete to the foundation of belief and faith that is essential to seeing results from study of The Master Key System. If you are anything like me, then you may go through moments or periods of complete doubt and frustration when studying The Master Key System. You may get so fed-up that you neglect it for a long time. I know, it happens. Read this when you get depressed and rest fully assured that you are not crazy or placing your bet on a long shot. What you read in The Master Key System is known by many to be true and sound. It is not pie-in-the-sky stuff—it is the real deal. Believe me, especially when just beginning, one needs to be reassured.

The rest of the book just about fell together. As you read The Master Key System, you see Mr. Haanel reference quite a few people: Judge Thomas Troward, James Allen, and Henry Drummond. I researched these people and found many of their writings. The writings I excerpted here were pieces that I found to be poignant, insightful, and influential, in the sense that you can see how Haanel was influenced. A few pieces were written after The Master Key System was published, but they illustrated some of Haanel's thoughts and ideas so perfectly that I just had to include them.

If you care to read more from the illustrious authors that I included in Master Key Arcana, their books can be found in libraries, bookstores, and even online. It is my hope that you expand what you read in this book and learn everything that you can about the science of the mind and mind stuff. What is contained here is but a drop in the ocean of what is available. It is your choice to dive into that ocean and probe the depths.

I have been working as much as possible to piece together a more in-depth biography of Charles F. Haanel. It has been slow-going. There is not much known or written about the man. I spoke to a couple of his descendants and they barely knew that their great-grandfather was a writer, let alone one who was so influential! The best biography I have of Mr. Haanel is included in this book. The images of his interment certificate and obituary were compliments of a dedicated researcher named Dwight A. Radford of NGS NewsMagazine. I think that you will find these items to be of interest as they "humanize" Haanel.

In the back of this book, you will see other images of quite a few things: original correspondence materials, marketing materials, and covers. I hope these will give you a historical perspective on the man and his books. They're also just pretty neat.

The last item in this books is a poem by Rudyard Kipling, "If." It is a poem that I read for inspiration and guidance; it also fits well with the tone of the other writings in this book. I have absolutely no clue if Mr. Kipling was influenced by or familiar with Haanel. Frankly, I doubt that he was. But there is no doubt that this little poem of his encapsulates perfectly the teachings of Haanel. I sincerely hope that you read this poem often and garner as much as I have from it.

It is my intention with this book to supply you with material that will assist you as you study The Master Key System course. Thank you for allowing me to do that. If you are becoming newly acquainted with Charles F. Haanel and The Master Key System, then I sincerely hope and wish that you explore fully that amazing tome and achieve success beyond your wildest wishes. Remember: You have the tools; Haanel supplies the instruction manual.

Have fun... Tony.
June, 2004

Charles F. Haanel– A Biography

In St. Louis–History of the Fourth City (S. J. Clarke Publishing Co., St. Louis, 1909) by Walter B. Stevens, this is what was written about Charles F. Haanel.

Charles F. Haanel is largely associated with the business interests of the city, being affiliated with a number of enterprises of acknowledged financial worth. Beside being president of the Continental Commercial Company he is also president of the Sacramento Valley Improvement Company and president of the Mexico Gold & Silver Mining Company. Mr. Haanel is in every sense of the word a self-made man, having risen in the commercial world to his present station of worth and prominence by the utilization of his own natural resources.

Born in Ann Arbor, Michigan, May 22, 1866, he is the son of Hugo and Emeline (Fox) Haanel, who removed with him to St. Louis when he was in early childhood. He initiated himself into the business world as an office boy for the National Enameling & Stamping Company. For this company he worked for a period of fifteen years.

Finally he resigned his position with this firm and being ambitious to rise higher in the financial world, he conceived the idea of organizing a company for the purpose of promoting an enterprise. At that time the vicinity of

Tehuantepec, Mexico, was reputed as being especially adapted to the growth of sugar and coffee. He succeeded in convincing a number of capitalists of the feasibility of taking up land in that section of the country and working a plantation. The land was purchased and the company organized to engage in the raising of sugar and coffee. Of this company he was made president.

The plantation was successful from the beginning and soon became an enterprise of considerable financial worth. This was organized in 1898 and in 1905 Mr. Haanel organized the Continental Commercial Company, which was consolidated with the other company and also absorbed six additional companies. It is now operating under the name of the Continental Commercial Company with Mr. Haanel as president. It is capitalized for two million five hundred thousand dollars, and is one of the largest of its kind in the world.

Mr. Haanel has by no means confined his efforts to these lines, however, but has extended his labors to other enterprises with which he is associated in a prominent capacity. He was one of the organizers of the Sacramento Valley Improvement Company and from the beginning has been its president. Since its inception the company has enjoyed an era of prosperity and now owns and controls the largest Tokay vineyards in the world. He is likewise president of the Mexico Gold & Silver Mining Company, a company of some importance in developing the rich mineral resources of the southern republic.

In 1885 Mr. Haanel was united in marriage with Miss Esther M. Smith. Sixteen years later he was left a widower with one son and two daughters, and in July, 1908, he was married to Miss Margaret Nicholson of St. Louis, a daughter of W. A. Nicholson.

While Mr. Haanel is a Republican, his pressing business interests have given him no time to take an active interest in politics beyond that of casting his vote and using his influence for the election of the candidates of the party in whose principles he firmly believes.

He is a member of Keystone lodge, a thirty-second degree Mason and a Shriner. He is also affiliated with the Missouri Athletic Club.

He is a man of mature judgment, capable of taking a calm survey of life and correctly valuing its opportunities, its possibilities, its demands and obligations. He has wisely sought success along the lines of least resistance and yet when difficulties and obstacles have confronted him he has displayed a force of character that has enabled him to overcome them and continue on the pathway to prosperity. Many a man whose life is one of untiring industry does not win success for he lacks the complement to industry a laudable ambition which prompts the individual to reach out into other fields and eagerly grasp the opportunities that are presented. In these qualities Mr. Haanel is richly endowed and has thus attained his present enviable position in financial circles.

Mr. Haanel died on November 27, 1949 at the age of 83. He was buried in Bellefontaine Cemetery, St. Louis.

During his life, Mr. Haanel earned and received many degrees, including hon. Ph.D., College National Electronic Institute; Metaphysics, Psy. D., College of Divine Metaphysics; and M.D., Universal College of Dupleix, India.

Mr. Haanel was also affiliated with many groups, including Fellow London College of Psychotherapy; member Authors' League of America; American Society of Psychical Research; member of the Society of Rosicrucians; the American Suggestive Therapeutical Association; Science League of America; Pi Gamma Mu Fraternity; Master Mason, Keystone Lodge No. 243, A.F. & A.M.; created a Noble in Moolah Temple.

G-D 12-1-1949

C. F. Haanel, Retired Author, Buried

Funeral services were held yesterday for Charles F. Haanel, retired businessman and author, who died Sunday of heart disease at his home, 7129 Cornell ave., University City.

Haanel, 80, wrote several volumes on subjects such as the correct method of thinking, after a varied career in business. Among Haanel's works was "The Master Key System" on thought and concentration.

Haanel was associated with an enameling firm here, was in the sugar business in Mexico, and headed a grape growing company in California.

Surviving are his wife and two daughters, Mrs. Charles Frees of St. Louis and Mrs. Chester M. Hawke of San Marino, Cal.

Burial was in Bellefontaine Cemetery.

An obituary for Charles F. Haanel.
(Thanks to Dwight A. Radford for finding this.)

2M 1944

THIS ORDER MU[...]ATION FOR BURIAL

HAANEL, CHARLES FRANCIS — 7129 Cornell, Sun., Nov. 27, 1949, husband of Margaret Nicholson Haanel.
Private service was held at Lupton Chapel, Wed., 10 a. m. Interment Bellefontaine Cemetery.

St. Louis, Nov 28, 1949.

Secretary **Bellefontaine Cemetery Association,**

You are hereby authorized to inter the remains of Charles F. Haanel. Age 83.

In Lot No. #4646 Block No. #6. In Name of C. F. Haanel.

Relationship of Deceased to Lot Owner Owner.

Funeral on Wednesday Nov the 30/49 at 11:00 o'clock A. M., at Cemetery Grounds.

Open Grave Remaining space in front of Monument.

(GIVE LOCATION ON DIAGRAM ON OTHER SIDE)

Sign Here Mrs Chas F Haanel (Relationship) wife
(READ NOTICE BELOW)

7129 Cornell Ave. (Relationship)

Vault

Box Norwalk Concrete Box.

SPECIAL NOTICE—If lot owner is dead, state relationship to him or her of signer of this order, otherwise it will not be accepted.

If a grave marker for this interment is ordered from a monument company, this order will be construed as our authorization to permit same to be erected, unless the contrary is expressly stated on this order.

Charles F. Haanel's interment certificate, signed by his wife.
(Thanks again to Dwight A. Radford for finding this.)

Part Twenty-five

The Hidden Manna

1. We live in a fathomless sea of plastic mind substance. This substance is ever alive and active. It is sensitive to the highest degree. It takes form according to mental demand. Thought forms the mould or matrix from which the substance expresses. Our ideal is the mould from which our future will emerge.

2. The Universe is alive. In order to express life there must be mind; nothing can exist without mind. Everything that exists is some manifestation of this one basic substance from which and by which all things have been created and are continually being recreated. It is man's capacity to think that makes him a creator instead of a creature.

3. All things are the result of the thought process. Man has accomplished the seemingly impossible because he has refused to consider it impossible. By concentration, men have made the connection between the finite and the Infinite, the limited and the Unlimited, the visible and the Invisible, the personal and the Impersonal.

4. The building up of Matter from Electrons has been an involuntary process of individualizing intelligent energy.

5. Men have learned a way to cross the ocean on floating palaces; how to fly in the air; how to transmit thought around the world on sensitized wires; how to cushion the earth with rubber and thousands of other things just as remarkable, just as startling, and just as incomprehensible to the people of a generation ago.

6. Men will yet turn to the study of life itself and with the knowledge thus gained will come peace and joy and length of days.

7. The search for the elixir of life has always been a fascinating study and has taken hold of many minds of Utopian mould.

In all times, philosophers have dreamed of the day when man will become the master of matter. Old manuscripts contain many, many receipts that have cost their inventors bitter pangs of baffled disillusionment. Thousands of investigators have laid their contributions upon the sacrificial altar for the benefit of mankind.

8. But not through quarantine or disinfectants or boards of health will man reach the long-sought plane of physical well-being; nor by dieting or fasting or suggesting will the Elixir of Life and the Philosopher's Stone be found.

9. The Mercury of the Sages and the "hidden manna" are not constituents of health foods.

10. When man's mind is made perfect, then—and then only—will the body be able perfectly to express itself.

11. The physical body is maintained through a process of continuous destruction and reconstruction.

12. Health is but the equilibrium that nature maintains through the process of creating new tissue and eliminating the old, or waste, tissue.

13. Hate, envy, criticism, jealousy, competition, selfishness, war, suicide, and murder are the causes that produce acid conditions in the blood, causing changes that result in irritation of the brain cells, the keys upon which Soul plays "Divine Harmonies" or fantastic tricks before high heaven, according to the arrangement of chemical molecules in the wondrous laboratory of nature.

14. Birth and death are constantly taking place in the body. New cells are being created by the process of converting food,

water, and air into living tissue.

15. Every action of the brain and every movement of the muscle means destruction and consequent death of some of these cells; and the accumulation of these dead, unused, and waste cells is what causes pain, suffering, and disease.

16. We allow such destructive thoughts as fear, anger, worry, hatred, and jealousy to take possession and these thoughts influence the various functional activities of the body, the brain, the nerves, the heart, the liver, or the kidneys. They in turn refuse to perform their various functions: the constructive processes cease and the destructive processes begin.

17. Food, water, and air are the three essential elements necessary to sustain life, but there is something still more essential. Every time we breathe, we not only fill our lungs with air, but we fill ourselves with Pranic Energy, the breath of life replete with every requirement for mind and spirit.

18. This life-giving spirit is far more necessary than air, food, or water. A man can live for forty days without food, for three days without water, and for a few minutes without air; but he cannot live a single second without Ether. It is the one prime essential of life, so that the process of breathing furnishes not only food for body building, but food for mind and spirit as well.

19. It is a well known fact in India, but not so well-known in this country, that in normal, rhythmical breathing, exhalation and inhalation takes place through one nostril at a time: for about one hour through the right nostril and then for a like period through the left nostril.

20. The breath entering through the right nostril creates positive

electromagnetic currents, which pass down the right side of the spine; while the breath entering through the left nostril sends electromagnetic currents down the left side of the spine. These currents are transmitted by way of the nerve centers—or ganglia—of the sympathetic nervous system to all parts of the body.

21. In the normal, rhythmical breath, exhalation takes about twice the time of inhalation. For instance, if inhalation requires four seconds, exhalation, including a slight natural pause before the new inhalation, requires eight seconds.

22. The balancing of the electro-magnetic energies in the system depend to a large extent upon this rhythmical breathing, hence the importance of deep, unobstructed, and rhythmic exhalation and inhalation.

23. The wise men of India knew that with the breath, they absorbed not only the physical elements of the air, but life itself. They taught that this primary force of all forces, from which all energy is derived, ebbs and flows in rhythmical vibration through the created universe. Every living thing is alive by the virtue of partaking of this cosmic breath.

24. The more positive the demand, the greater the supply. Therefore, while breathing deeply and rhythmically in harmony with the universal breath, we contact the life force from the source of all life in the innermost parts of our being. Without this intimate connection of the individual soul with the great reservoir of life, existence as we know it would be an impossibility.

25. Freedom does not consist in the disregard of a governing principle, but in conformity to it. The laws of Nature are infinitely just. A violation of just law is not an act of freedom.

The laws of Nature are infinitely beneficent. Exception from the operation of a beneficent law is not freedom. Freedom consists in conscious harmonious relation with the Laws of Being. Thus only may desire be satisfied, harmony attained, and happiness secured.

26. The mighty river is free only while it is confined within its banks. The banks enable it to perform its appointed function, and to answer its beneficent purpose to the best advantage. While it is under the restraint of freedom, it gives out its message of harmony and prosperity. If its bed is raised, or its volume greatly increased, it leaves its channel and spreads over the country, carrying a message of ruin and desolation. It is no longer free. It has ceased to be a river.

27. Necessities are demands, and demands create action, which result in growth. This process makes for each decade a larger growth. So it is truly said that the last twenty-five years have advanced the world more than any previous century, and the last century has advanced the world more than all the ages of the past.

28. Notwithstanding all of the different characters, dispositions, and idiosyncrasies of different people, there is a certain definite law which dominates and governs all existence.

29. Thought is mind in motion, and psychic gravity is to the law of the mind what atomic attraction is to physical science. Mind has its chemistry and constituent powers and these powers are as definite as those of any physical potency.

30. Creation is the power of mind, by which the thought is turned inward and made to impregnate and conceive new thought. It is for this reason that only the enlightened mind can think for itself.

31. The mind must acquire a certain character of thought, which will enable it to reproduce them itself without any seed from without to impregnate it.

32. When mind has acquired this nature, it is able to spontaneously generate thoughts without outside stimulation.

33. This is done by conceiving thought in the mind as a result of being impregnated and fecundated by the Universal.

34. They must not be permitted to go out into space, but on the contrary, must remain within where they will create psychic states corresponding to their natures.

35. It is this absorption of self-generated thoughts and their conception of corresponding psychic states that is the Principle of Causation.

36. This is possible owing to the fact that the mental Cosmos is perpetually radiated as a Unity of Mind, and this Mind functions in connection with the soul of man as his mind.

37. It being essence, it is identified with the essence of the Cosmos, and with the essence of all things.

38. The result is, that having attained unto and having become an Infinity of thought, the individual is Omniscient in Mind, Omnipotent in Will, and Omnipresent in Soul. The quality of his mind is Omniscience and the quality of his soul is Omnipresence.

39. Such a man is possessed with real power in all that he does. He is indeed a Master, the Creator of his own destiny, the arbiter of his own fate.

40. There are many flowers of varicolored blossoms. Each blossomed stem simply reaches up to the great sun—the god of vegetable life manifestation—without complaining, without doubt, and in all the fullness of plant desire, faith, and expectancy.

41. They demand and attract the richness of color and perfume. And so man will, too, in the future unshackle the great desire forces of mind and soul and turn them to heaven in righteous demand for the highest gift in the Universe: Life.

42. And life means to live. Age is a prejudice, which has become so firmly anchored in your mind that any casual number of years mentioned evokes a precise image on your brain.

43. Twenty years, you see a youth or a young girl adorned with all of the juvenile graces.

44. Thirty years, a young man or young woman in the full development of vital strength and equilibrium, still on the up-grade towards the dazzling heights of maturity.

45. Forty years, the summit has been reached, the effort made having been maintained by the prospect of the vast horizons to be dominated.

46. The road traversed is contemplated with pride, but with emotion you already turn towards the abyss whose dizzy curves wind steeply into ever-increasing darkness.

47. Fifty years, half-way down the slope, which is still illumined by the light from the peaks though already touched by the chill of the abyss. An organism weakened and compelled to submit to numerous abdications.

48. Sixty years brings you to the entrance of the cold melancholy valleys. Resigned to inexorable destiny you stand on the threshold of old age. You begin preparations for the long journey that must inevitably be undertaken.

49. Seventy years wrinkled and old endowed with numerous infirmities, you sit in the waiting-room for the last journey considering it miraculous that you are still alive.

50. If the eightieth year is exceeded, the fact is mentioned as an amazing phenomenon and you are treated with the respect due to antiquities.

51. Is this parallel correct? Is there any connection between age and age value? Let it be emphatically stated that the tyranny of the birth certificate can be abolished.

52. The fact that a year represents one complete revolution of the earth round the sun has nothing in common with the evolution of the human being.

53. To be so many years old means simply that the circling seasons have been observed so many times, and nothing more. It implies no consideration of the intellectual or physical state. The person who has seen the untiring astronomical phenomenon forty times may be much younger in the real meaning of the word than one who has seen it but thirty times.

54. The vibratory activities of the planetary Universe are governed by a law of periodicity. Everything that lives has periods of birth, growth, and fruitage. These periods are governed by the Septimal Law.

55. The law of Sevens governs the days of the week, the phases of the moon, the harmonies of sound, light, heat, electricity,

magnetism, atomic structure. It governs the life of individuals and of nations, and it dominates the activities of the commercial world. We can apply the same law to our own lives and therefore come into an understanding of many experiences which would otherwise appear inexplicable.

56. Life is growth and growth is change. Each seven year period takes us into a new cycle.

57. The first seven years is the period of infancy. The next seven the period of childhood, representing the beginning of individual responsibility. The next seven represents the period of adolescence. The fourth period marks the attainment of full growth. The fifth period is the constructive period, when men acquire property, possessions, a home and family. The next, from 35 to 42, is a period of reactions and changes, and this in turn is followed by a period of reconstruction, adjustment and recuperation, so as to be ready for a new cycle of sevens, beginning with the fiftieth year.

58. The law of periodicity governs cycles of every description. There are cycles of short periods, and cycles of long periods. There are periods when the emotions gain the ascendancy and the whole world is absorbed in religious thought; and there are other periods when science and learning take the ascendancy and the patent office is flooded with new inventions. There are other periods when vice and crime rule with a high hand; periods of strikes and hard times, times of turmoil, confusion and disaster; and there are periods of reform.

59. What is the cause of these cycles? Are they arbitrary, have they no basis or foundation in nature, recurring with almost the regularity of clockwork and without any incentive whatever? Or are they perhaps due to Universal Laws, and caused by the revolution of the planets in their orbits, having their

origin in some principle in nature which man may learn and thus ultimately be able to predict with certainty the recurrence of the same phenomena?

60. Let us consider the division of the Zodiac into four grand quarters resembling: Spring, Summer, Autumn, and Winter. The Spring Quarter corresponds to infancy, childhood, and youth; the irresponsible and educational period from the first to the twenty-first year of life, when the personal is being fitted by service and study for the next important stage. It is the time when fidelity and filial reverence, obedience, and industry are instilled into the growing mind.

61. The Summer Quarter of life from 21 to 42 is the practical period of life, and is concerned with the life of the householder, in which wealth becomes an object, responsibility grows, and the duties of life become heavier and filled with business activity. It is the period when the social side of the personality is expressed and the lesson of unselfishness is learned; prosperity comes with the fullness of life which abounds in the Summer portion. The virtues developed are caution, thrift, charity, magnanimity, diligence, and prudence.

62. This period of life is governed by the sign, Leo, in which the life forces burn at their greatest heat, and love for partner and offspring finds its greatest height in the domestic and social world.

63. The Autumn Quarter of life is one in which the glory of manhood and the fullness of motherhood are turned to wider interest, and personal claims are sacrificed for the benefit of those outside the narrow circle of the home. The duties of government and the national welfare are taken up with motives that are less limited and more altruistic in their nature, the desire being to help in the ruling and guiding of those

who belong to the nation. The virtues to be acquired are equilibrium, justice, strength, courage, vigour, and generosity.

64. The concentralising power of this period is denoted by the sign Scorpio, symbol of self-controlled emotions, fixed feelings, and permanent modes of action—the fluidity and changeable sensations of the watery signs being made stable and reliable and fixed.

65. The next stage of life is the period in which experience is garnered and the lessons of life are stored ready for the enriching of the Ego. It is the stage in which the review of life brings wisdom and the tender feelings of sympathy to all; the virtues of the last three signs are made manifest as patience, self-sacrifice, service, purity, wisdom, gentleness, and compassion.

66. The centralising of the mind in the sign Aquarius brings the climax when the Man is complete and the humanized perfection of manhood culminates in the one whose mind is wholly centered in higher states of consciousness.

67. This is the plan of the normal evolution of humanity, when the civilized nations have worked through their infantile, spring-like stage. For nations, like individuals, are also evolving, and it is the national good and the national perfection that is to be the outcome of this wisely ordained plan, in accordance with the will of the Supreme Ruler of the Universe.

68. Perhaps it was this national good and national perfection which one of our great men saw, when he had the wonderful vision, which he so beautifully described.

69. "A vision of the future arises. I see a world where thrones have crumbled and where kings are dust. The aristocracy of idleness has perished from the earth.

70. "I see a world without a slave. Man at last is free. Nature's forces have by science been enslaved. Lightning and light, wind and waves, frost and flames, and all the subtle powers of the earth and air are the tireless toilers for the human race.

71. "I see a world at peace, adorned with every form of art, with music's myriad voices thrilled, while lips are rich with words of love and truth; a world in which no exile sighs, no prisoner mourns; a world on which the gibbet's shadow does not fall; a world where labor reaps its full reward, where work and worth go hand in hand.

72. "I see a world without the beggar's outstretched palm, the miser's heartless stony stare, the piteous wail of want, the livid lips of lies, the cruel eyes of scorn.

73. "I see a race without disease of flesh or brain—shapely and fair, married harmony of form and function—and, as I look, life lengthens, joy deepens, love canopies the earth; and over all, in the great dome, shines the eternal star of faith."[†]

† The philosopher whom Haanel is quoting is Robert Green Ingersoll (1833-1899) from his piece "A Vision of War."

Thought

With every strong thought, with every earnest longing
For aught thou deemest needful to thy soul,
Invisible vast forces are set thronging
Between thee and that goal.

'Tis only when some hidden weakness alters
And changes thy desire, or makes it less,
That this mysterious army ever falters
Or stops short of success.

Thought is a magnet; and the longed for pleasure
Or boon, or aim, or object, is the steel;
And its attainment hangs but on the measure
Of what thy soul can feel.

—Author Unknown†

† The author is Ella Wheeler Wilcox (1850-1919) and the poem is "Thought-Magnets" from her collection of poems, "Poems of Power" (c. 1901).

The Missing Parts of
The Master Key System

Part Twenty-six

The Bridge of Life

1. Life is not created–it simply is. All nature is animate with this force we call "Life." The Phenomena of Life on this physical plane, with which we are chiefly concerned, are produced by the involution of "energy" into "matter." Matter is itself an involution of energy.

2. Living tissue is organized–or organic–matter. Dead tissue is unorganized–or inorganic–matter. When life disappears from an organism, disintegration begins.

3. Organization requires a high rate of vibration, or short wave lengths, moving with great intensity. The molecules of which the tissue is composed are in a continuous state of activity. The result is the tissues manifest what we call "life."

4. Senility is a part of the death process. It is caused by an accumulation of Earthy salts, or so-called mineral matter.

5. This mineral matter usually consists of lime and chalk that settle upon the walls of the arteries. The arteries then become hardened and calcinous and lose their elasticity.

6. If the vibrations are sufficiently intense, it would be impossible for these salts to settle in the system. The intense vibration would make the accumulation impossible. The minerals would be expelled in the process of elimination.

7. Old age, decay, and death are therefore simply due to the inability of the individual to keep in tune with the source of all life.

8. Life is a rate of vibration–a mode of motion. Death is the absence of that vibration.

9. Life is a manifestation of activity. Death is the process of disin-

tegration—the absence of activity.

10. The Earth is ever seeking to embrace in its bosom all things. It is the tomb or fixed resting place for every form of organized manifestation.

11. The vibrations from the Earth are, therefore, the vibrations of destruction and disintegration. Nothing has so far been able to resist the continual pull of these Earthy vibrations. Everything has had to finally succumb. All form of whatever nature has thus far been compelled to return to the Earth to await the vitalizing vibrations of the Sun before being again brought into manifestation.

12. Will this always be true? Not necessarily. It may not always be necessary to contact these disintegrating vibration. We may be able to insulate ourselves to some extent at least.

13. The Universe was built by vibration. That is to say, the specific form that everything has, on either a large or a small scale, is due absolutely to the specific rate of vibration that gave expression to it. The Universe, then, both in general and in particular, is the effect of a system of vibration. In other words, the music of the spheres has expressed itself in that form, which we denominate the "Cosmos."

14. This vibration expresses intelligence. This is not intelligence as we understand the word, but a cosmic knowledge that is responsible for the growth of finger nails, hair, bones, teeth, and skin; the circulation of blood; and breathing. All of these proceed whether we are asleep or awake.

15. Thus, consciousness or intelligence abounds in every thing, peculiar to itself only in that it differs in character to every other thing, for there is but one Universal Consciousness or

Intelligence, while there are multitudinous different expressions of it. The rock, the fish, the animal, the human are all recipients of the one Universal Intelligence. They are only differently formed manifestations of Cosmic substance–differently combined rates of motion or vibration.

16. Mind is a system of vibration. The brain is a vibrator. Thought is the organized effect of each particular vibration when expressed through the requisite combination of cells.

17. It is not the number of cells, but their vibratory adaptability that gives range to the thoughts of which the mind is capable.

18. It is through the Universal Mind that the Seeds of Thought enter the brain of man, so that it conceives thought, which becomes a current of Energy–centripetal in the mind of man and centrifugal in the Universal Mind.

19. These seeds of thought have a tendency to germinate, to sprout, and to grow. They thus form what we call ideas.

20. When a mental picture is formed in the brain, the rate of vibration corresponding to that picture is immediately awakened in the ether. It depends, however, upon whether the Will or Desire principle is acting as to whether that vibration moves inward or outward.

21. If the Will is used, the vibration moves outward and the principle of force is put into operation. If the Desire nature is awakened, the vibrations move inward and the Law of Attraction is put into operation.

22. In either case, the Law of Causation expresses itself through the embodying or Creative Principle.

23. The time is not far distant when man will be able to make the body immune against disease and arrest the ordinary process of old age and physical decay—perpetuate youth even after the body has passed the mark of the centuries.

24. Immortality, or perpetual life, is the fondest hope, the legitimate goal, and the just birthright of every human being. But the majority of people of all religions—and those of no religious beliefs at all—seem to think that it is to be obtained, if at all, at some future time and on some other plane of existence.

25. Every human being who is not sick or insane has an innate desire to live as long as possible. If there is an individual person in the world who does not desire to live, it is because he is in some abnormal condition of body or mind, or he expects to be.

26. As a matter of fact, the more highly enlightened and developed the individual, the more intense the desire and longing for life, and it is improbable that there would be a natural desire for something that was impossible for attainment.

27. Prof. Jaques Loeb, formerly of the Department of Physiology at the University of California, said several years ago, "Man will live forever when he has learned to establish the right protoplasmic reaction in the body."

28. Thomas Edison says, " I have many reasons to believe that the time will come when man will not die."

29. Five-sevenths of the flesh and blood are water, while the substance of the body consists of albumen, fibrin, casein, and gelatin. That is, it consists of organic substance composed originally of four essential gases: oxygen, nitrogen, hydrogen, and carbonic acid.

30. Water is a combination of two gases. Air is a mixture of three gases. Thus, our bodies are composed of only transformed gases. None of our flesh existed three or four months ago—face, mouth, arms, hair, and even the very nails.

31. The entire organism is but a current of molecules, a ceaselessly renewed flame, a stream at which we may look all of our lives and never see the same water again.

32. These molecules do not touch each other and are continuously renewed by means of assimilation, which is directed, governed, and organized by the immaterial force that assimilates it.

33. To this force we may give the name "soul," so writes the great French Astronomer, Physicist, Biologist, and Metaphysician Camille Flammarion.

34. The Bridge of Life, a symbol of physical regenesis, has been exploited in song, drama, and story. Paracelsus, Pythagoras, Lycurgus, Valentin, Wagner, and a long unbroken line of the Illuminati from time immemorial have chanted their epics in unison with this "riddle of the Sphinx," across the scroll of which is written, "Solve me or die."

35. This solution may lie in an understanding of the nature of the glands that control physical and mental growth, and all metabolic processes of fundamental importance.

36. These glands dominate all the vital functions and cooperate in an intimate relationship, which may be compared to an interlocking directorate.

37. They furnish the internal secretions—or hormones—that determine whether we are to be tall or short, handsome or

homely, brilliant or dull, cross or congenial.

38. Sir William Osler, one of the world's great thinkers, said, "For man's body is a humming hive of working cells each with its specific functions, all under central control of the brain and heart, and all dependent on secretions from the glands which lubricate the wheels of life. For example, remove the thyroid gland, just below the Adam's Apple, and you deprive man of the lubricants which enable his thought-engines to work, and gradually the stored acquisitions of his mind cease to be available, and within a year he sinks into dementia. The normal processes of the skin cease, and the hair falls, the features bloat, and the paragon of animals is transformed into a shapeless caricature of humanity."

39. There are seven major glands: the pituitary; the thyroid; the pancreas; the adrenal; the pineal; the thymus; and the sex glands. All of which control the metabolism of the body and dominate all vital functions.

40. The pituitary is a small gland located near the center of the head, directly under the third ventricle of the brain, where it rests in a depression in the floor-plate of the skull. Its secretions have an important part in the mobilizing of carbohydrates, maintaining blood pressure, stimulating other glands, and maintaining the tonicity of the sympathetic nervous system.

41. The thyroid gland is located at the frontal base of the neck, extending upward in a sort of semicircle on both sides. The thyroid secretion is important in mobilizing both proteids and carbohydrates; it stimulates other glands; helps resist infections; affects the hair growth; and influences the organs of the digestion and elimination. It is a strongly determining factor in the all-around physical development and also in the mental

functioning. A well-balanced thyroid will insure an active, efficient, and smoothly coordinated mind and body.

42. The adrenal glands are located just above the small of the back. These organs have sometimes been called the "beauty glands," since one of their functions is to keep the pigments of the body in proper solution and distribution. But of greater importance is the agency of the adrenal secretion in other directions. The secretions contain a most valuable blood-pressure agent and are a tonic to the sympathetic nerve system, hence to the involuntary muscles, heart, arteries, and intestines. These glands respond to certain emotional excitements by an immediate increase in volume of secretion, thus increasing the energy of the whole system and preparing it for effective response.

43. The pineal gland is a small conical structure located behind the third ventricle of the brain. The ancients realized that this gland was of vast importance and was spoken of as a "spiritual center," the seat of the soul, and possibly of eternal youth or life everlasting. It is near the top and at the back of the head.

44. The thymus gland is located at or near the bottom of the throat, just below the thyroid gland. It is considered essential for children only, but is it not possible that the degeneration of this gland is one of the causes of premature senility?

45. The pancreas is located just behind the peritoneum near the stomach. This gland aids digestion and when not properly functioning, an excess of sugar may be produced, which causes diabetes and other serious troubles.

46. The sex glands are located at the lower part of the abdomen. It is through the functioning of these glands that life is created and the process of reproduction is carried on.

47. When the secretions from these glands are not called upon for procreative purposes, they are poured into the cell life, renewing the energy, strength, and vitality.

48. If they fail to function, there is depression and general debility.

49. It is clear then, that if we can find some way to make these glands continue to function, we can renew our health, strength, and youth indefinitely. This is so because the thyroid develops vital energy; the pituitary controls blood pressure and develops mental energy; the pancreas controls digestion and bodily vigor; the adrenals furnish pep and ambition; and the sex glands control the secretions that manifest as youth, strength, and power.

50. We can better understand the mechanism of glands when we remember that the rays from the Sun are differentiated into seven different tones or colours or qualities by the seven different planets and that they enter the human system by the seven plexi located along the spinal column. We now find that this life is carried to the seven major glands in the body, where it controls and dominates every function of life.

51. Unfortunately, however, ordinary window glass excludes practically all of the ultra-violet rays, which are the most essential in the maintenance of health and vitality. A few sanitariums and hospitals have had special windows of fused quartz constructed, which admits these ultra-violet rays.

52. When the glands are supplied with the ultra-violet rays, of which we have heretofore been deprived, the result will be a remarkable degree of vitality–mental and physical vigor. In fact, it is already known that cholesterol can be converted into a vitamin by the action of the ultra-violet rays, and it is

possible that other inert substances may be activated in a like manner.

53. The ultra-red rays have also been found to be an exceedingly valuable therapeutic agent. Fabrics of certain weaves are used to filter these rays.

54. Deductions from the experiments made by several of the world's leading scientists more than fifteen years ago are to the effect that it will be possible for the physical body of man to become so purified and responsive that it may continue living from age to age without death. The income and outgo of the body can be so perfectly adjusted that the organism will not become old, but will be rebuilt from day to day.

55. The vibratory force of Life can be inspired to such a degree and radiated through the tissues to such an extent that this man of clay will really become a temple of the living God, not merely a reservoir of unconscious and unregulated intelligence.

56. By very simple hygienic care, we can greatly prolong each life manifestation. Hence, we have reason to believe that a complete knowledge of vibratory force and its effect upon the structure of the body will aid the organism in making the life manifestations permanent.

57. Death is not a necessary, inevitable consequence or attribute of life. Death is biologically a relatively new thing, which made its appearance only after living things had advanced a long way on the path of evolution.

58. Single celled organisms have proved, under critical experimental observation, to be immortal. They reproduce by simple fission of the body, one individual becoming two. This

process may go on indefinitely without any permanent slacking of the rate of cell division and without the intervention of a rejuvenating process, provided the environment of the cells is kept favourable. The germ cells of all sexually differentiated organisms are, in a similar sense, immortal. Reduced to a formula, we may say that the fertilized ovum produces a soma and more germ cells. The soma eventually dies. Some of the germ cells prior to that event produced somata and germ cells, and so on in a continuous cycle that has never yet ended since the appearance of multi-cellular organisms on the earth.

59. So long as reproduction goes on in this way in these multi-cellular forms, there is no place for death.

60. The successful cultivation of the tissues of higher vertebrates over an indefinitely long period of time demonstrates that death is in no sense a necessary concomitant of cellular life.

61. It may fairly be said that the potential immortality of all essential cellular elements of the body either has been fully demonstrated or has been carried for enough to make the probability very great. Generalizing the results of the tissue culture work of the last two decades, it is highly probable that the cells of all the essential tissues of the metazoan body are potentially immortal, as is shown when placed separately under such conditions as to supply appropriate food in the right amount and to remove promptly the deleterious products of the metabolism.

62. A fundamental reason why the higher multi-cellular animals do not live forever appears to be that in the differentiation and specialization of function of cells and tissues in the body as a whole, any individual part does not find the conditions necessary for its continued existence. In the body, any part is dependent for the necessities of its existence, upon other

parts, or upon the organization of the body as a whole. It is the differentiation and specialization of function of the mutually dependent aggregate of cells and tissues that constitute the metazoan body that brings about death, and not any inherent or inevitable mortal process in the individual cells themselves.

63. When cells show characteristic senescent changes it is probably a consequence of their mutually dependent association in the body as a whole. It does not primarily originate in any particular cell because of the fact that the cell is old. It occurs in the cells when they are removed from the mutually dependent relationship of the organized body as a whole. In short, death does not appear to be a primary attribute of the physiological economy of individual cells as such, but rather of the body as a whole.

64. Recent researches have shown conclusively that tissues and cells in the human body need not necessarily decay. Formerly it was thought that there was no way to ward off senility and that cells are bound to break down due to old age, which simply means wear and tear. This, however, in the light of modern science, is no longer countenanced. The study of gland science has convinced many physicists that the human cells can be rejuvenated or replaced continuously and that such a thing as old age can be warded off for several hundred years.

65. It is well known that it takes a lifetime to gain valuable experience. Men at the head of great industries frequently are over sixty years of age and their advice is sought because they have gained most valuable experience during all those years. It would seem, therefore, important to lengthen the span of life, and indeed, present indications are that this can and will be done.

66. Some of our best authorities see no reason why a human

being should not attain the age of several hundred years. Not as some extraordinary feat, but considered as a fair average. There are, of course, people now living who are 125 years old, but these are, of course, exceptions. Medical scientists assert that the goal of 200 years will be reached some day in the future. When we stop to think that the average life-time used to be 40 years and that now we consider the man of 50 years to be in the prime of his life, who knows but that in fifty years hence a man in his prime will be 100 or 150 years of age.

67. Dr. Monroe, an eminent physician and scientist of Great Britain, says, "The human frame as a machine contains within itself no marks by which we can possibly predict its decay. It is apparently intended to go on forever."

68. The nerves are fine threads of different colours, each one having a special chemical affinity for certain organic substances, such as oil or albumen, through and by which the organism is materialized and the process of life carries on.

69. The imagination might easily conceive that these delicate infinitesimal fibres are strings of the Human Harp and that the molecular minerals are the fingers of Infinite Energy striking the notes of some Divine Anthem.

70. But of all the multiple adepts or masters that have kept the light burning above the Three Piers of the Magical Bridge, none has more clearly and beautifully written thereof than did the great poet, Isaiah:

71. "Then the eyes of the blind shall be opened, and the ears of the deaf shall be unstopped. Then shall the lame man leap as a hart, and the tongue of the dumb shall sing; for in the wilderness shall waters break out, and streams in the desert. And the glowing sand shall become a pool, and the thirsty

ground springs of water. In the habitation of jackals, where they lay shall be grass of reeds and bushes. And a highway shall be there, and a way and it shall be called, 'The Way of Holiness.' The unclean shall not pass over it, but it shall be for the redeemed. The wayfaring man, yea, fools, shall not err therein."

The View

Looked on the World with a Care-lined frown
Mottled and grey were the shaded ways;
Anger and Avarice, Envy and Hate,
Clouded the view of the sun-draped days.

Looked on the World with a Soulful Song,
Zephyrs blew sweet o'er the Hills of Time;
Wafted the Peace I had longed for long–
Sundrift aglow on the fields of Thyme.

Follow the thought and thought sublime
Shines through the dark and the darkness fades
Thoughts are the things that control the chimes
Of the Bells that Ring in the Golden Glades.

–Nate Collier

The Missing Parts of
The Master Key System

Part Twenty-seven

The Elimination of Fear

1. Your emotions will invariably seek to express themselves in action. The emotion of love will therefore seek expression in demonstrations of loving service.

2. Emotions of hate will seek expression in vindictive or hostile actions.

3. Emotions of shame will seek expressions in actions corresponding to the nature of the cause that brought the emotion into being.

4. Emotions of sorrow will bring the tear ducts into violent action.

5. From this you will see that the emotions always focalize the energies upon the idea or desire that is seeking an outlet.

6. When the emotions find an outlet through the proper channel, then all is well; but if they are forbidden or repressed, then the desire or wish will continue to gather energy and if, for any reason it is finally suppressed, it will pass into the subconscious, where it will remain.

7. Such a suppressed emotion becomes a complex. Such a complex is a living thing–it has vital power and force and the vital force retains its intensity undiminished throughout the entire life-time unless it is released. In fact, it gains in violence with every similar thought, desire, wish, or memory.

8. The emotion of love causes the solar plexus to become active, which in turn influences the action of glands, which produce a vibratory effect on certain organs of the body, which creates passion. The emotion of hate causes an acceleration of certain bodily activities, which change the chemical organization of the blood and eventuates in semi-paralysis or, if long continued, in complete paralysis.

9. Emotions may be expressed through mental, verbal, or physical action and they usually find expression in one of these three ways and are therefore released and this energy is dissipated in a few hours; but when by reason of honour, pride, anger, hatred, or bitterness these emotions are buried from consciousness, they become mental abscesses in the subconscious realm and cause bitter suffering.

10. Such a complex may find reverse expression. For instance, a man who has been forbidden to express his love for a woman may develop into a woman-hater. He may be irritated and annoyed by the sight of feminine things. He may appear to be bold, independent, and dominant, but this will be but the camouflage by which he is attempting to cover up the craving for love and sympathy that has been denied him.

11. Should this man eventually select a mate, he will unconsciously select one of an opposite type to the one who caused him sorrow. The attachment has been reversed—he wants no reminders.

12. Suffering is an emotion and it opens the doors of the subconscious mind. The thought, "This is what I get for wrong-doing," produces a conclusion, "Well, I'll never do it again!" This is the reformation suggestion that goes down into the subconscious mind by the auto-suggestion of the individual suffering penance. Thus, reformation takes place because it changes the soul's desire and also produces a new desire to avoid the consequences of suffering indicated to it by the penance.

13. Desire originates in the subconscious mind. It is plainly an emotion. Emotion originates in the soul or subconscious mind. Pleasure emotions are the diversions and rewards for service that the subconscious mind renders the body.

14. You have seen that when any thought, idea, or purpose finds its way into the subconscious through the emotions, the sympathetic nervous system takes up the thought, idea, or purpose and carries it to every part of the body, thus converting the idea, thought, or purpose into an actual experience in your life.

15. The necessary interaction of the conscious and subconscious mind requires a similar interaction between the corresponding system of nerves. The cerebrospinal system is the channel through which we receive conscious perception from the physical senses and exercise control over the movements of the body. This system of nerves has its center in the brain.

16. Any explanation of the phenomena of life must be based upon the theory of Oneness. The psychic element being found within all living substances—this Cosmic Intelligence—must have existed before living substance could have come into existence and therefore it exists today all around us, flowing in and through us. This Cosmic Consciousness projects itself in the form of living substance and it acts with a conscious intelligence in manufacturing its food supply and evolving organizations on to a higher and higher plane of life.

17. This Cosmic Mind is the Creative Principle of the Universe—the Divine Essence of all things. It is, therefore, a subconscious activity and all subconscious activities are governed by the sympathetic nervous system, which is the organ of the subconscious mind.

18. No human intelligence has ever accomplished the results that the Cosmic Intelligence produced in developing a chemical laboratory right within the foundation of plant life, and the production of elaborate mechanical devices and harmonious social organization right within our own bodies.

19. In the mineral world, everything is solid and fixed. In the animal and vegetable kingdom, it is in a state of flux—forever changing and always being created and recreated. In the atmosphere we find heat, light, and energy. Each realm becomes finer and more spiritual as we pass from the visible to the invisible, from the coarse to the fine, and from the low potentiality to the high potentiality. When we reach the invisible, we find energy in its purest and most volatile states.

20. And as the most powerful forces of Nature are the invisible forces, so we find that the most powerful forces of man are his invisible forces—his spiritual force. The only way in which the spiritual force can manifest is through the process of thinking.

21. Addition and subtraction are, therefore, spiritual transactions; reasoning is a spiritual process; ideas are spiritual conceptions; questions are spiritual searchlights; and logic, argument, and philosophy are spiritual machinery.

22. Every thought brings into action certain physical tissue, parts of the brain, nerve, or muscle. This produces an actual physical change in the construction of the tissue. Therefore, it is only necessary to have a certain number of thoughts on a given subject in order to bring about a complete change in your physical organization.

23. Thoughts of courage, power, and inspiration will eventually take root and as this takes place, you will see life in a new light. Life will have a new meaning for you. You will be reconstructed and filled with joy, confidence, hope, and energy! You will see opportunities to which you were heretofore blind. You will recognize possibilities that before had no meaning for you. The thoughts with which you have been impregnated are radiated to those around you and they in

turn help you onward and upward. You attract to yourself new associates and this in turn changes your environment. By the simple exercise of thought, you change not only yourself, but your environment, circumstances, and conditions.

24. These changes are brought about by the psychic element of life. This psychic element is not mechanical. Because of its power of selection, organization, and direction, such a power can not be automatically mechanical.

25. The Cosmic Intelligence possesses the function of memory for the purpose of recording all the experiences that it encounters and projecting and organizing itself on higher planes of life. It is this function of memory that is the hereditary directing force found within living organisms.

26. This hereditary directing force frequently manifests as fear. Fear is an emotion. It is consequently not amenable to reason. You may therefore fear your friends as well as your enemies or fear the present and past as well as the future. If fear attacks you, it must be destroyed.

27. You will be interested in knowing how to accomplish this. Reason will not help you at all, because fear is a subconscious thought–a product of the emotion. There must then be some other way.

28. The way is to awaken the Solar Plexus. Get it into action. If you have practiced deep breathing[†], then you can expand the abdomen to the limit. That is the first thing to do. Hold this breath for a second or two, then still holding it, draw in more air and carry it to the upper chest and draw in the abdomen.

† Read "The Amazing Secrets of the Yogi" by Charles F. Haanel, which is also published by Kallisti Publishing, to learn the proper method of breathing.

29. This effort flushes the face red. Hold this breath also for a second or two and then, still holding your breath, deflate the chest and expand the abdomen again. Do not exhale this breath at all, but, still holding it, alternately expand the abdomen and chest rapidly some four or five times. Then exhale. The fear is gone.

30. If the fear does not leave you at once, repeat the process until it does. It will not be long before you are feeling entirely normal. Why? Because in the first place, this breathing effort concentrated at the pit of the stomach affects the great ganglion of the sympathetic nervous system lying exactly opposite. This is the Solar Plexus, which largely governs circulation.

31. The stimulation of the Solar Plexus releases the nerve currents and the renewed circulation re-establishes the muscular control.

32. The breath entering through the right nostril creates positive electro-magnetic currents, which pass down the right side of the spine; while the breath entering through the left nostril sends negative electro-magnetic currents down the left side of the spine. These currents are transmitted by way of the nerve centers or ganglion of the sympathetic nervous system.

33. We may be said to literally live, move, and have our being, in a physical sense, in the sun. This force or energy enters the etheric spleen with every inhalation of the breath. As it enters the spleen, the solar plexus draws it to itself with every exhalation, and from the solar plexus it travel along the nerves to the sacral plexus situated at the extreme end of the spine, and to the cardiac plexus, the core of the brain. These are the three main centers of the body.

34. From the cardiac plexus, this life energy traverses the nerves

to the head. Again on the downward path, it passes through to the psychic center. Then it traverses the nerves of the face; then the bronchial center; the throat front; the pulmonary center; the upper chest and the lungs; the lower lung center, which is seated above the heart; the vital and generative center seated at the base of the stomach; and so this life energy makes the circuit of nerves until it gradually works its way out through the pores of the skin.

35. You will, therefore, readily see why this exercise can and does completely eliminate that arch enemy, Fear.

36. If you are tired, if you wish to conquer fatigue, then stand still wherever you may be with your feet holding all your weight. Inhale deeply and raise the body to the tip toes with the hands stretched above the head and the fingers pointed upward. Bring your hands together above the head, inhaling slowly and exhaling violently. Repeat this exercise three times. It will only take a minute or two and you will feel more refreshed than you would if you took a nap. In time, you will be able to overcome the tendency to fatigue.

37. The virtue of this exercise is in the intention. The intention governs the attention. This in turn acts upon the imagination. The imagination is a form of thought, which in turn is mind in motion.

38. All thought formations interact upon one another until they come to a state of maturity, where they reproduce their kind. This is the law of creation. These are indicated in the characteristics of the individual. If the body is large, the bones heavy, the finger nails thick, and the hair coarse, then we know that the physical predominates. If the body is slight, the bones small, and the finger nails thin and pliable, then we know that the mental and spiritual characteristics prevail.

Coarse hair indicates materialistic tendencies. Fine hair indicates sensitive and discriminating mental qualities. Straight hair indicates directness of character. Curly hair indicates changefulness and uncertainty in thought.

39. Blue eyes indicate a light, happy, cheerful, active disposition. Grey eyes indicate a cool, calculating, determined disposition. Black eyes indicate a quick, nervous, venturesome disposition. Brown eyes indicate sincerity, energy, and affection.

40. You are, therefore, a complete manifestation of your most inward thoughts. The colour of your eyes, the texture of your skin, the quality of your hair, and every line and curve of your body are indications of the character of the thoughts that you habitually entertain.

41. Not only this, but the letters that you write carry not only the message that the words contain, but they are charged with an energy corresponding with the nature of your thought and therefore often bring a very different message than the one that you intended to send.

42. And finally, even the clothes that you wear eventually take on the mental atmosphere that surrounds you, so that the trained psychometrist finds no difficulty in reading the character of those who have worn a garment for any length of time.

Part Twenty-eight

The Gift of the Gods

1. In an ordinary bar of iron or steel, the molecules arrange themselves promiscuously in the body. The magnetic circuits are satisfied internally and there is no resulting external magnetism.

2. When the bar is magnetized, the molecules rearrange themselves according to the law of attraction: they turn on their axis and assume positions more nearly in a straight line with their north ends pointing the same way. The closed magnetic circuits are thus broken up and external magnetism is made evident.

3. You cannot see the molecules of iron or steel changing their relative positions under the influence of magnetism, but the effect reveals that change that has taken place. When all of the molecules have turned on their axis until they are all arranged symmetrically, the bar has been completely magnetized. It cannot be further influenced, however strong the force.

4. The bar has now become a magnet and will exert force in every direction. The amount of force that the magnet will exert decreases as the distance from the magnet increases.

5. The magnetic lines complete their circuits independently and never cut, cross, or merge into each other.

6. Another bar of iron or steel placed in the magnetic field of a magnet assumes the properties of the magnet. This phenomenon is known as magnetic induction. This is the action and reaction that always precedes the attraction of a magnet for a magnetic body.

7. Electricity is the invisible agent known to us only by its various manifestations. You are a perfect electrical plant. Food, water,

and air furnish the fuel; the solar plexus is the storage battery; and the sympathetic nervous system is the medium by which the body is charged with magnetism. Sleep is the process by which the battery is recharged and the vital processes replenished and renewed.

8. The male is the positive, or electrical, charge and the female is the negative, or magnetic, charge. The male represents current, force, and energy. The female represents capacity, resistance, and power.

9. What happens when one of the opposite sex comes into your magnetic field? First, the Law of Attraction is brought into operation. Then, by the process of induction, you are magnetized and assume the properties of the person whom you are contacting.

10. When another person enters your magnetic field, what is it that passes from one to the other? What causes the thrill and tingle over the entire sympathetic nervous system? It is the cells rearranging themselves so as to carry the charge of energy, life, and vitality that is passing from one to the other, which you are receiving by the process of induction. You are being magnetized and in this process you are assuming the qualities and characteristics of the person whom you are contacting.

11. In the magnetism that is passing from person to person is all the joy, all the sorrow, all the love, the hatred, the music, the art, the fear, the suffering, the success, the defeat, the ambition, the triumph, the reverence, the courage, the wisdom, the virtue, and the beauty that heredity and environment have stored in the life of your love. For it is nothing less than love: the Law of Attraction is the Law of Love and Love is life and this is the experience by which life is being quickened into

action and by which character heredity and destiny are being determined.

12. When you become impregnated with these thoughts of love, success, ambition, triumph, defeat, sorrow, hatred, fear, or suffering, are you immediately conscious of them? By no means! Why not? The reply is very simple and easily understood: the brain is the organ of the conscious mind and it has five methods only by which it can contact the conscious world. These methods are the five senses: seeing, hearing, smelling, tasting, and feeling. But Love is something that we cannot see, we cannot hear; nor can we taste, smell, or touch it. It is therefore plainly a subconscious activity or emotion. The subconscious, however, has its own system of nerves whereby it contacts every part of the body and receives sensations from the outer world. The mechanism is complete; it controls all of the vital processes: the heart, the lungs, the digestion, the kidneys, the liver, and the organs of generation. Nature has evidently taken all of these out of the control of the conscious mind and placed them in the control of the more reliable subconscious, where there can be no interference.

13. Where physical contact is made, an entirely different situation is created. In this case, we bring into action the cerebrospinal nervous system also, through the sense of touch. You will remember that the conscious mind has five methods by which it contacts the outer world. The sense of touch is one of these and actual physical contact brings into action not only the sympathetic nervous system, but the cerebrospinal nervous system.

14. As the brain is the organ of this system of nerves, you immediately become conscious of any such action. So that when both the emotions and the feelings are aroused by both

mental and physical contact, we bring into action every nerve in the body.

15. The exchange resultant from these associations should be beneficial, inspiring, and vitalizing, and such is the case when the association is ideal and constructive. Such an association produces an effect in consciousness and life, typified by the increased power and usefulness in the crossing of plants, birds, and animals. This result means added power, utility, beauty, wealth, or worth.

16. The Principle of Attraction, as it operates through infinite time, evidences itself in the form of growth. The one fundamental and inevitable result of attraction is the bringing together of things that have an affinity for each other with a resultant eternally advancing growth of life.

17. You have found what happens when one of the opposite sex comes into your magnetic field. Now let us consider what happens when you approach another personality of the same sex.

18. All human intercourse is a matter of accommodation and you will be a factor in determining what the relationship shall be and it rests with you to determine whether you shall be the predominant factor in the new relationship.

19. If you give, then you are the positive, or predominant, factor.

20. If you receive, then you are the negative, or receptive, factor.

21. Each person is a magnet having both positive and negative poles and with tendencies that impel an automatic sympathy with or antipathy toward whatever approaches or is approached.

22. Normally, the positive poles lead the way and the approach of two positives from opposite directions foreshadows a collision.

23. The fundamental of life is harmony. Discords are obstructions that lie in your path. They obscure the reality of peace that lies at the heart of every experience, but as you increase in experience, you are enabled to discern the good in apparent evil and your power of attraction increases proportionately.

24. To the extent that you are magnetized toward "saturation point," you may determine your relation to others and their relation to you.

25. Any magnet has the power to induce harmonious conjunction with one that is less powerful.

26. This is accomplished by causing a reversal of polarity of one of the magnets. Then dissimilar poles come together in peace and harmony.

27. The more positive magnet will compel the less positive magnet to become receptive to the greater power that dominates it.

28. The lesser magnet may be obliged to be receptive to the overpowering influence. It acknowledges the impelling power that requires it to reverse its polarity.

29. It turns its positive pole away and its negative pole toward the positive pole of the greater magnet and the two meet in harmonious relation.

30. The negative magnet may, however, have the higher knowl-

edge and may not desire to dominate. Possessing greater wisdom, it may disdain the use of force.

31. Perhaps it prefers to conciliate or wishes to receive rather than give. Instead of forcibly obliging the lesser magnet to accommodate itself to imposed conditions, the greater magnet may voluntarily reverse its own polarity.

32. If you are a great soul you will know intuitively whether to exercise coercion or non-resistance. Where coercion is used, the resultant harmony is an involuntary and temporary submission; the non-resistant method binds because of the sense of freedom that it confers.

33. The coercive method is distinctively intellectual, while that of non-resistance is essentially spiritual.

34. If you are highly developed spiritually and similarly endowed with intellectual power, you can use the latter to the greatest advantage. In this case, you will neither discard reason or logic because in your understanding of life's mathematics you will make application of spiritual geometry, mental algebra, and physical arithmetic according to the requirements of your problem.

35. You will find that existence involves ever recurrent occasions for accommodation, compromise, and reversal of polarities. You may escape compulsion through acquiescent submission and avoid the use of force by inviting pleasurable acquiescence.

36. You may command and exact unwilling obedience or you may invite and receive voluntary cooperation.

37. You may induce harmonies and create friendships or you

may plant hatreds that will react as obligations that must eventually be satisfied.

38. An understanding of the properties of the human magnet will enable you to solve many of the problems of life.

39. Conflict and opposition have their place, but ordinarily they constitute obstacles and pitfalls to be avoided.

40. You will find that you can always avoid useless opposition and unprofitable conflict by reversing your polarity or impelling its reversal in your would-be opponent.

41. You are, indeed, in the loving care of principles that are immutable and that are designed solely for your benefit.

42. You may place yourself in harmony with them and thus express a life of comparative peace and happiness, or you may put yourself in opposition to the inevitable with necessarily unpleasant results.

43. You determine your conscious relation to all that is. You express the exact degree of happiness or the reverse that you have earned through the associations that you have permitted to come into your life.

44. You may from any one experience learn the spiritual lesson it was intended to convey or you may make necessary many similar experiences.

45. You may gather wisdom from experience rapidly and with ease or you may do so slowly and with difficulty.

46. You are able to consciously control your conditions as you come to sense the purposes of what you attract and are able

to extract from each experience that which you require for further growth.

47. When you possess this faculty to a high degree, you may grow rapidly and reach planes of thought where opportunities for greater service await you. It remains for you on each successive plane to learn how to express the greater harmonies that your higher growth has placed within your reach, for it is only through expression that you may appropriate what is for your use or benefit.

48. You have now entered upon the borderland of the basic, the fundamental, the active principle of life. Little did you realize a few years ago the innumerable vibrations that surround you—such as electric, magnetic, heat, and actinic—the control and the use of which are now keeping you busy.

49. Suppose that what you term "electrons" should be active centers of intelligence connected with an Infinite Mind, which is all-wise and all-knowing. That marvelous mind that thinks with design and sees ends from beginning.

50. Suppose that "electrons" should not be centers of force and energy only, but centers of intelligence; and that mankind will finally discover that the brain is an organized center of millions of these intelligent electrons and that they are in contact with all other electrons of which the Universe is composed.

51. The Universe is an effect of a system of vibration. The Cosmos is organized by the action of energy vibrating in accordance with certain rates that express themselves in form. The Universe could, therefore, in no case be anywise different than it is unless the vibratory influence that organized it had been different, the Universe being the expression in form of those vibratory influences that have organized it out of the

Cosmic energy or ether.

52. Sir William Crooks took some very fine sand and scattered it over the head of a drum. Then by taking a tuning fork and sounding different notes just above the drum head so that the vibration set in motion by this particular key would vibrate upon the drum head, the sand was seen to shift and assume a definite geometrical figure corresponding to the particular note that was sounded.

53. When another note was sounded, the sand shifted and assumed another figure, demonstrating that the notes of a musical scale will produce a corresponding form in any substance sufficiently plastic to assume form under their direction.

54. This proves that vibration is the origin of form with each particular vibration giving rise to a corresponding form.

55. Vibration, then, is at the foundation of physics! Form, as well as light, heat, colour, and sound are inseparably connected with vibratory activities. Each vibration expresses itself in a form corresponding to that particular rate of vibration.

56. Form, then, is the organized result of energy at certain rates of vibration. Vibrations express themselves in corresponding geometrical figures and in this way build up crystals that are the expression of vibration with a number of these crystals collectively forming a body of the particular elements that is the outgrowth of that particular vibration.

57. Study the beautiful forms of snowflakes falling on cold winter days. You will find that one day the forms are quite different from those of the day before or the day after, although the conditions may differ but in the very smallest degree.

58. Nevertheless, this minute difference has sufficed to evolve these very different forms, each of which is the exact expression of a special complex relation between moisture, motion, pressure, temperature, rarity, electrical tension, and chemical composition of the air that prevailed during their formation.

59. When a thread is introduced into a bowl of saline solution and then lifted out of it, there will gather over the entire length of the submerged string a mass of mathematically perfect crystals of salt.

60. It has been observed by the students of nature that the crystals are never exactly alike. Not only is this true of the different chemical elements, but we know that each individual crystal is a little different. Now, knowing that this crystallization is due to vibration and all differences in the form of the crystal are, therefore, due to differences in the rates of vibration, we can recognize the fact that the individuality of any object is due to the corresponding individuality in the vibration that gave expression to it.

61. It is the law of vibration that brings to maturity the fruit of every thought, whether wholesome or unwholesome, desirable or undesirable. It is this law that causes the things that we see to take form; it is this law that gives sparkle to the diamond, lustre to the amethyst, colour to the grape, fragrance to the rose, and beauty to the lily; and it is through the operation of this law that each of us is attracting to ourselves the associates, experiences, circumstances, conditions, and environment by which we are related to the objects and purposes that we seek.

62. Existence is like the output of a loom. The pattern and the design is there; but whereas our looms are mere machines, once the guiding cords have been fed into them, the Loom of Time is complicated by a multitude of free agents who

can modify the web, making it the product more beautiful or more ugly according as they are in harmony or disharmony with the general scheme.

63. With the Arabic numerals–1, 2, 3, 4, 5, 6, 7, 8, 9, 0–any conceivable number may be expressed.

64. With the twenty-six letters of the alphabet, any conceivable thought may be expressed.

65. With the fourteen primary elements, any conceivable thing may be organized.

66. What is true in the inorganic world is likewise true in the organic: certain conscious processes will invariably be followed by the same consequence. Clearly, then, it requires an intelligent force to direct the activities of these electrons and cause them to unite with regular mathematical precision and thus bring into being matter of every conceivable form.

67. Mind is then the source of all things, in the sense that the activity of mind is the initial cause of all things coming into being. This is because the primal source of all things is a corresponding thought in the Universal Mind. It is the essence of a thing that constitutes its being and the activity of mind is the cause by which the essence takes form.

68. An idea is a thought conceived in the mind and this rational form of the thought is the root of form, in the sense that this form of thought is the initial formal expression that acting upon Substance causes it to form.

69. There can be nothing except as there is an idea, or ideal form, engendered in the Mind. Such ideas acting upon the Universal engender corresponding forms.

70. Matter being Cosmic Mind in physical manifestation, we perceive that everything is possessed of intelligence directing its development and manifestation. This is the intelligence that causes rocks to cohere and crystallize, while plants manifest life in an entirely different manner.

71. Plant life divides its cells rapidly and absorbs moisture, air, and light readily, while the rock expels them. But they both combine and transform elements in just the right proportions to reproduce, perpetuate, and colour their species.

72. The one purpose in life for centuries was as simple as that of the lower animals and plants: the simple aim of self-preservation and of the production of descendants. Human beings were contented with the simplest organic function, nutrition, and reproduction. Hunger and love were their only motives for action. For a long period, they must have aimed at the one single object of self-preservation.

73. In the route of our ancestry, specific lines were traveled and specific character established. We lose neither the one nor the other, for both lines and character are projected from generation to generation. The lines, although invisible, are never broken. Nor are they ever abruptly changed to other type expressions. Neither are the characteristics ever lost though they continue to project from generation to generation down through the ages.

74. We may distill, analyze, and compound all the elements that are used as conveyors or vehicles in the process of constructive energy and we will not find the element that will produce a nut, a plum, or even as much as a mustard seed, unless we send the energy into condensation over character lines as constructive moulds that must first be established.

75. Character lines are invisible tracks over which and through which Nature is ever pressing into constructivity every element and thing of creation from the plane of the fungi to that of the intellectual and Spiritual Man.

76. In the highest form of expression, the Principle of Attraction is expressed in love. It is the One Universal Principle that equally governs the seeming involuntary affinities of minerals and vegetable substances, the passions of animals, and the loves of men.

77. The Law of Love is a piece of pure science and the oldest and simplest form of Love is the elective affinity of two differing cells. Above all laws in the Law of Love, for Love is life.

78. Progress being the object of Nature and Altruism the object of Progress, the Book of Life is found to be a love story.

Mind is the Master power
That molds and makes;
And man is mind,
Who evermore takes
The tool of thought, and
Shaping what he wills,
Brings forth a thousand
Joys, a thousand ills;
He thinks in secret
And it comes to pass,
Environment is but
His looking glass.

—James Allen

The Master Key Psychological Chart

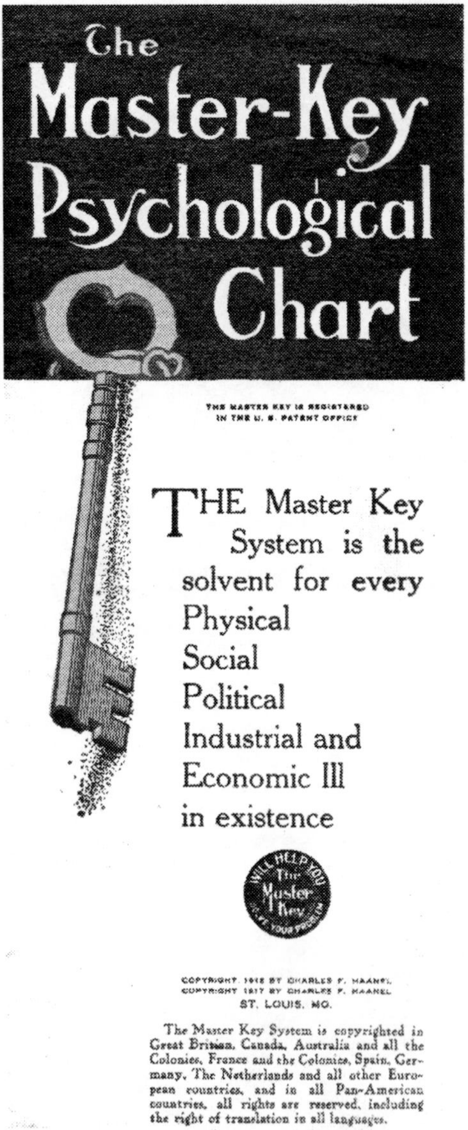

The
Master-Key
Psychological
Chart
THE MASTER KEY IS REGISTERED
IN THE U. S. PATENT OFFICE
THE Master Key
System is the
solvent for every
Physical
Social
Political
Industrial and
Economic Ill
in existence
WILL HELP YOU
The
Master
Key
COPYRIGHT 1916 BY CHARLES F. HAANEL
COPYRIGHT 1917 BY CHARLES F. HAANEL
ST. LOUIS, MO.
The Master Key System is copyrighted in Great Britian, Canada, Australia and all the Colonies, France and the Colonies, Spain, Germany, The Netherlands and all other European countries, and in all Pan-American countries, all rights are reserved, including the right of translation in all languages.

This is a pamphlet or marketing brochure that Haanel used to advertise The Master Key System. It included the Psychological Chart and readers' letters of praise for the System. The last copyright on it is 1917. The back cover containing the "List of Publications" is located in the "Images of Original Material" section of this book.

The Master Key Psychological Chart

It is a psychological fact that ninety percent of our mental power is never or seldom used. Therefore, most men have the power to achieve ten times as much as they ever accomplish.

This chart will tell you exactly where you stand, what you are accomplishing, and what you can accomplish if you make the necessary effort. Fill this in.

Mental Product	__%
Health	__%
Time Efficiency	__%
Creative Power	__%
Concentration	__%
Total	__%
Divide by 5—Average	__%

Mental Product

The first test is your Mental Product. What is it worth? Are you cashing in on it? Are you getting full value for it? What you get for your mental product depends entirely upon your ability to sell it to the best advantage. The chances are that many men with no more ability than yourself are cashing in ten, twenty, or fifty times more than you are for a product no better than yours. If so, there is a reason, and this chart will explain it.

Estimate the value of what you have to sell—your knowledge, your experience, your loyalty, your energy—and if you are marketing it at its full rate value give yourself 100%. If you are only getting one-half of what it is worth give yourself 50%. But be fair. Do not underestimate the value of what you have to offer. Remember that loss leads to greater loss and most loss comes from self-depreciation. Cause and effect do not operate somewhere, sometimes; but everywhere, always. This is an invariable law, so that whatever we receive, good or bad, is the result of a definite cause and reaches us either as a penalty or a reward.

And remember this: Your ability to cash in on your mental product at the rate of 5% annually on a half million dollars does not depend upon ability or knowledge either. You may be selling your product for $2,000 a year and it may be more valuable than that of many who are cashing in at the rate of $25,000 a year. The reason is plain. Knowledge does not apply itself! You are allowing it to remain in static form—you must convert it into dynamic form by applying creative power and concentration. The lack of concentrated, intelligent, charted effort may be costing you $20,000 a year.

Health

Next, take Health. If you eat well, sleep well, take a reasonable amount of recreation, and can attend to your business, profession, or household duties without any consideration for or thought of the state of your health, give yourself 100%. But if your body needs constant attention or if you have to be continually worried about what to eat or what not to eat, if you cannot sleep, or if you have aches or pains of any description, then deduct from the 100%. If you think your health is 90% or if you are only 50% efficient, then put it down. Be absolutely fair!

Remember that your physical body is maintained through a process of continuous destruction and reconstruction. Life is simply an exchange of the old for the new and health is only the equilibrium that nature maintains during the process of creating new tissue and eliminating the old (or waste) tissue.

Birth and death are constantly taking place in our body. New cells are constantly being formed by the process of converting food, water, and air into living tissue. Every action of the brain and every movement of a muscle means the destruction and consequent death of some of these cells. The accumulation of these dead, unused, and waste cells is what causes pain, suffering, and disease. The symptoms depends upon what organs are being taxed in their effort to eliminate the waste matter.

An understanding of these laws and a consequent knowledge as to how to preserve an equilibrium between the new cells that are being created and the old cells that are being eliminated is the secret of perfect health.

Time Efficiency

Next in importance comes Time Efficiency, because time is all that we have and what we accomplish depends entirely upon what use we make of our time. If you work eight hours; sleep eight hours; and use eight hours for recreation, study and self-improvement; and all the time is fully utilized, then give yourself 100%.

But if any part of the eight hours which should be sold at a profit is spent in idleness or gossip or any form of mental dissipation; if any part of this time is wasted or worse than wasted by allowing your thought to rest on critical, discordant, or inharmonious subjects of any kind; then cut your percentage accordingly. If you fall asleep the minute your head touches the pillow, all right; but if you spend from 15 minutes to an hour trying to get to sleep, cut your percentage down again. If your sleep is disturbed by dreams or fear or worry of any kind, cut your percentage down again.

If you jump up early and feel refreshed and vigorous, you bathe and make your toilet without the loss of any unnecessary time, then well and good; but if you idle or dream or fritter away, then cut your percentage down again. If you spend the rest of your time in good healthy recreation that benefits you both physically and mentally, then well and good—you are acquiring capital which will have a cash value; but if you let the time get away form you with nothing to show for it, if you are not better physically, mentally, or morally, if the time has gone and left nothing which you can cash in, nothing of value, then it has been lost and possibly worse than lost for it may leave something detrimental—something that will prove a handicap in your race for success. Here again you must be fair with yourself and give yourself exactly the percentage to which you are entitled.

Creative Power

Next comes your Creative Power. If most persons whom you meet do what you want them to do; if they feel toward you as you wish them to feel; if they think what you want them to think, then give yourself 100%, because everything we get must come from others. There is no other channel by which success can reach us. This creative power must be unconsciously exercised—it must be your personality. If, however, you have to make a tremendous effort when you wish to accomplish something, if you have to exert will power, if you must fret and worry and stew over the result of an important interview, then cut your percentage down to 50% or 40% or even less, because you do not understand the principle involved.

When you understand, there will be no cause for anxiety—you will know. Because in the first place you will never want or expect anyone to do anything except what is best for them. You will understand that every transaction must benefit both parties. When you understand these laws, when the principles become a vital part of your life, when they are involved in your mental attitude, you will have found the Master Key and all doors will be open to you because you will understand that every event, every condition, every thing was first an idea, and that just to the extent that you grew quiet and focused your attention on that idea, stilling all the activities of the mind and eliminating all other thoughts from your consciousness, will the various phases and possibilities of the idea develop. And just in accordance with the definiteness with which you picture that idea and the extent with which the idea takes possession of you will the creative power do its work and the creative power will eventually take control and direct every activity of both mind and body and will begin to shape every condition related to the idea so that sooner or later the idea will come forth in definite tangible form. If you understand this thoroughly and have demonstrated it time and time again so that you can mould and shape and determine conditions, then give yourself 100%.

Concentration

Next comes Concentration. Can you concentrate? Do you know what it means to concentrate? Can you direct the thought to any problem that may arise for five minutes, ten minutes, or fifteen minutes to the absolute exclusion of everything else? Can you unravel, disintegrate, take the problem apart, see every phase of it, see the cause which brought it about, see the solution, see it definitely, conclusively, and finally, and know that your solution is correct? Can you then dismiss the matter and turn your attention to something else without ever recurring to the matter again? If you can do this, then give yourself 100%. If, however, you are haunted by fears, troubles, anxieties; if, when you have no problem to solve, you make one for yourself by drawing on your imagination; if you are afraid of what this one says or the other one thinks or someone else does, then cut down your percentage because if you know how to concentrate you would not be afraid of anyone or anything. You would be in possession of a power which would make every other known power sink into insignificance. Be careful to give yourself exactly the percentage to which you feel you are entitled.

Now strike an average. See where you stand. If you are a little above the average, your chart will be something like this:

Mental Product	50%
Health	80%
Time Efficiency	80%
Creative Power	50%
Concentration	10%
Total	270%
Divide by 5–Average	54%

Assuming you are earning $5,000 a year and that you feel that your mental product should be worth $10,000 a year, which is the basis for your calculation, then any method which would assist you to increase your earning power to $10,000 a year would be worth $5,000 a year to you.

Again any method that would bring you health, efficiency in your time, efficiency in your creative power, or increase your ability to concentrate, would be worth at least $5,000 a year. Many have found that the Master Key System does all of this and much more.

The Master Key is a system of applied metaphysics. According to the New Standard Dictionary, "Metaphysics is the reasoned doctrine of the essential nature and fundamental relations of all that is real." Metaphysics is, therefore, a very practical science.

Let us see what are the most powerful forces in Nature. In the mineral world, everything is solid and fixed. In the animal and vegetable kingdom, it is in a state of flux–forever changing, always being created and recreated. In the atmosphere we find heat, light, and energy. Each realm becomes finer and more spiritual as we pass from the visible to the invisible, from the coarse to the fine, and from the low potentiality to the high potentiality. When we reach the invisible, we find energy in its purest and most volatile state.

And as the most powerful forces of Nature are the invisible forces, so we find that the most powerful forces of man are his invisible forces—his spiritual force—and the only way in which the spiritual force can manifest is through the process of thinking. Thinking is the only activity that the spirit possess and thought is the only product of thinking.

Addition and subtraction are therefore spiritual transactions. Reasoning is a spiritual process. Ideas are spiritual conceptions. Questions are spiritual searchlights. And logic, argument, and philosophy are spiritual machinery.

Every thought brings into action certain physical tissue: Parts of the brain, nerve, or muscle. This produces and actual physical change in the construction of the tissue. Therefore it is only necessary to have a certain number of thoughts on a given subject in order to bring about complete change in the physical organization of man.

This is the process by which failure is changed to success. Thoughts of courage, power, inspiration, and harmony are substituted for thoughts of failure, despair, lack, limitation, and discord. And as these thoughts take root, the physical tissue is changed and the individual sees life in a new light—old things have actually passed away, all things have become new, he is born again, this time born of the spirit, life has new meaning for him, he is reconstructed and is filled with joy, confidence, hope, and energy. He sees opportunities for success to which he was heretofore blind. He recognizes possibilities that before had no meaning for him. The thoughts of success with which he has been impregnated are radiated to those around him and they in turn help him onward and upward. He attracts to him new and successful associates and this in turn changes his environment. So that by this simple exercise of thought, a man changes not only himself, but his environment, circumstances, and conditions.

You will see—you must see!—that we are at the dawn of a new day. That the possibilities are so wonderful, so fascinating, so limitless as to be almost bewildering. A century ago, any man with an aeroplane or even a Gatling gun could have annihilated a whole army equipped with the implements of warfare then in use. So it is at present. Any man with a knowledge of the possibilities of modern metaphysics has an inconceivable advantage over the multitude.

The Master Key

Part I

Before any environment, successful or otherwise, can be created, action of some kind is necessary. And before action is possible, there must be thought of some kind, either conscious or unconscious. And as thought is a product of mind, it becomes evident that Mind is the creative center from which all activities proceed.

It is not expected that any of the inherent laws that govern the modern business world as it is at present constituted can be suspended or repealed by any force on the same plane, but it is axiomatic that a higher law may overcome a lower one. Tree law causes the sap to ascend, not by repealing the law of gravity, but by surmounting it.

To control circumstances, a knowledge of certain scientific principles of mind-action is required. Such knowledge is a most valuable asset. It may be gained by degrees and put into practice as fast as learned. Power over circumstances is one of its fruits. Health, harmony, and prosperity are assets upon its balance sheet. It costs only the labour of harvesting its great resources.

The naturalist who spends much of his time in observing visible phenomena is constantly creating power in that portion of his brain set apart for observation. The result is that he becomes very much more expert and skillful in knowing what he sees and grasping an infinite number of details at a glance than does his unobserving friend. He has reached this facility by exercise of his brain. He deliberately chose to enlarge his brain power in the line of observation, so he deliberately exercised that special faculty over and over with increasing attention and concentration. Now we have the result—a man learned in the lore of observation far above his fellows. Or, on the other hand, one can, by stolid inaction, allow the delicate brain matter to harden and ossify until his whole life is barren and fruitless.

Every thought tends to become a material thing. Our desires are seed thoughts that have a tendency to sprout and grow and blossom and bear fruit. We are sowing these seeds every day. What shall the harvest be? Each of us today is the result of his past thinking. Later we shall be the result of what we are now thinking. We create our own character, personality, and environment by the thought which we originate or entertain. Thought seeks its own. The law of mental attraction is an exact parallel to the law of atomic affinity. Mental currents are as real as electric, magnetic, or heat currents. We attract the currents with which we are in harmony. Are we selecting those which will be conducive to our success? This is the important question.

Lines of least resistance are formed by the constant action of the mind. The activity of the brain reacts upon the particular faculty of the brain employed. The latent power of the mind is developed by constant exercise. Each form of its activity becomes more perfect by practice. Exercises for the development of the mind present a variety of motives for consideration. They involve the development of the perceptive faculties, the cultivation of the emotions, the quickening of the imagination, the symmetrical unfoldment of the intuitive faculty (which without being able to give a reason frequently impels or prohibits choice) and finally the power of the mind may be cultivated by the development of the moral character.

"The greatest man," said Seneca, "is he who chooses right with invincible determination." The greatest power of the mind, then, depends upon its exercise in moral channels and therefore requires that every conscious mental effort should involve a moral end. A developed moral consciousness modifies consideration of motives and increases the force and continuity of actions. Consequently, the well-developed symmetrical character necessitates good physical, mental, and moral health, and this combination creates initiative, power, resistless force, and necessary success.

It will be found that Nature is constantly seeking to express Harmony in all things and is forever trying to bring about an harmonious adjustment for every discord, every wound, every difficulty. Therefore, when thought is harmonious, nature begins to create the material conditions, the possession of which are necessary in order to make up an harmonious environment.

When we understand that mind is the great creative power, what does not become possible? With Desire as the great creative energy, can we not see why Desire should be cultivated, controlled, and directed in our lives and destinies? Men and women of strong mentality who dominate those around them and often those far removed from them, really emanate currents charged with power which, coming in contact with the minds of others, causes the desires of the latter to be in accord with the mind of the strong individuality. Great masters of men possess this power to a marked degree. Their influence is felt far and near and they secure compliance with their wishes by making others "want" to act in accord with them. In this way men of strong Desire and Imagination may—and do—exert powerful influence over the minds of others, leading the latter in the way desired. The magnetic persons attract, allure, and draw. They are emotional and capture the will of others.

No man is ever created without the inherent power in himself to help himself. The personality that understands its own intellectual and moral power of conquest will certainly assert itself. It is this truth that an enfamined world craves today. The possibility of asserting a slumbering intellectual courage that clearly discerns and a moral courage that grandly undertakes is open to all. There is a divine potency in every human being.

We speak of the sun as "rising" and "setting", though we know that this is simply an appearance of motion. To our senses, the Earth is apparently standing still, and yet we know it is revolving rapidly. We speak of a bell as a "sounding body", yet we know that all that the bell can do is produce vibrations in the air. When these vibrations come at the rate of 16 per second they cause a sound to be heard in the mind. It is possible for the mind to hear vibrations up to the rate of 38,000 per second. When the number increases beyond this, all is silence again; so that we know that the sound is not in the bell, it is in our own mind.

We speak and even think of the sun as "giving light", yet we know it is simply giving forth energy that produces vibrations in the ether at a rate of four hundred trillion (400,000,000,000,000) per second causing what are termed light waves; so that we know that what we call "light" is simply a mode of motion and the only light that there is is the sensation caused in the mind by the motion of these waves. When the number of vibrations increases, the light changes in colour, each change in colour being caused by shorter and more rapid vibrations; so that although we speak of the rose as being red, the grass as being green, or the sky as being blue, we know that these colours exist only in our minds and are the sensation experienced by us as the result of the vibrations of light. When the vibrations are reduced below four hundred trillion per second, they no longer affect us as light, but we experience the sensation of heat.

So we have come to know that appearances exist for us only in our consciousness. Even time and space become annihilated. (Time being only the experience of succession, there being no past or future except as a thought relation to the present.) In the last analysis, therefore, we know that one principle governs and controls all there is. Every atom is forever conserved. Whatever is parted with must inevitably be received somewhere. It cannot perish and it only exists for use. It can go only where it is attracted and, therefore, required. We can receive only what we give and we may give only to those who can receive and it remains with us to determine our rate of growth and the degree of harmony that we shall express.

The laws under which we live are designed solely for our advantage. These laws are immutable and we cannot escape from their operation. All the great eternal forces act in solemn silence, but it is in our power to place ourselves in harmony with them and thus express a life of comparative peace and happiness.

Difficulties, inharmonies, and obstacles indicate that we are either refusing to give out what we no longer need, or refusing to accept what we require. Growth is attained through an exchange of the old for the new, of the good for the better. It is a conditional (or reciprocal) action, for each of us is a complete thought entity and the completeness makes it possible for us to receive only as we give. We cannot obtain what we lack if we tenaciously cling to what we have.

The Principle of Attraction operates to bring to us only what may be to our advantage. We are able to consciously control our conditions as we come to sense the purpose of what we attract and are able to extract from each experience only what we require for our further growth. Our ability to do this determines the degree of harmony or happiness we attain.

The ability to appropriate what we require for our growth continually increases as we reach higher planes and broader visions, and the greater our ability to know what we require, the more certain we shall be to discern its presence, to attract it, and to absorb it. Nothing may reach us except what is necessary for our growth. All conditions and experiences that come to us do so for our benefit. Difficulties and obstacles will continue to come until we absorb their wisdom and gather from them the essentials of further growth. That we reap what we sow is mathematically exact. We gain permanent strength exactly to the extent of the effort required to overcome our difficulties.

The inexorable requirements of growth demand that we exert the greatest degree of attraction for what is perfectly in accord with us. Our highest happiness will be best attained through our understanding of and conscious cooperation with natural laws.

Our mind-forces are often bound by the paralyzing suggestions that come to us from the crude thinking of the race, and which are accepted and acted upon without question. Impressions of fear, of worry, of disability, and of inferiority are given to us daily. These are sufficient reasons in themselves why men achieve so little—why the lives of multitudes are so barren of results, when all the time there are possibilities within them that need only the liberating touch of appreciation and wholesome ambition to expand into real greatness.

Women, perhaps more than men, have been subject to these conditions. This is true because of their finer susceptibilities making them more open to thought-vibrations from other minds, and because the flood of negative and repressive thoughts has been aimed more especially at them.

But it is being overcome. Florence Nightingale overcame it when she rose in the Crimea to heights of tender sympathy and executive ability before unknown young women. Clara Barton, the head of the Red Cross, overcame it when she wrought a similar work in the armies of the Union. Jenny Lind overcame it when she showed her ability to command enormous financial rewards while at the same time gratifying the passionate desire of her nature and reaching the front rank of her day in musical art. And there is a long list of women singers, philanthropists, writers, and actresses who have proved themselves capable of reaching the greatest literary, dramatic, artistic, and sociological achievement.

Women as well as men are beginning to do their own thinking. They have awakened to some conception of their possibilities. They demand that if life holds any secrets, these shall be disclosed. At no previous time has the influence and potency of thought received such careful and discriminating investigation. While a few seers have grasped the great fact that mind is the universal substance, never before has this vital truth penetrated the more general consciousness. Many minds are now striving to give this wonderful truth definite utterance. Modern science has taught us that light and sound are simply different intensities of motion, and this may lead to discoveries of forces within man that could not have been conceived of until this revelation was made.

A new century has dawned and now, standing in its light, man sees something of the vastness of the meaning of life—something of its grandeur. Within that life is the germ of infinite potencies. One feels convinced that man's possibility of attainment cannot be measured—that boundary lines to his onward march are unthinkable. Standing on this height, he finds that he can draw new power to himself from the infinite energy of which he is a part.

Part II

Some men seem to attract success, power, wealth, and attainment with very little conscious effort. Others conquer with great difficulty. Still others fail altogether to reach their ambitions, desires, and ideals. Why is this so? Why should some men realize their ambitions easily, others with difficulty, and still others not at all? The cause cannot be physical, else the most perfect men, physically, would be the most successful. The difference, therefore, must be mental—must be in the mind. Hence, mind must be the creative force and must constitute the sole difference between men. It is mind, therefore, that overcomes environment and every other obstacle in the path of men.

It is the actualizing of interior quality through the creative power of thought that has given us great leaders like Alexander, Napoleon, Cromwell, and our own Washington; captains of industry like Carnegie, Morgan, Rockefeller, and Harriman; inventors like Stevenson, Morse, Marconi, Edison, Tesla, and hosts of others. If, then, the only difference between men lies in their ability to think, to use and control their thought, to develop it—if the secret of all success, all power, all attainment is the creative power of mind, the force of thought—surely the ability to think correctly should become the paramount object of every man.

When the creative power of thought is fully understood, its effects will be seen to be marvelous. But such results cannot be secured without proper application, diligence, and concentration. The student will find that the laws governing in the mental and spiritual world are as fixed and infallible as in the material world. To secure the desired results, then, it is necessary to know the law and to comply with it. A proper compliance with the law will be found to produce the desired result with invariable exactitude. The student who learns that power comes from within, that he is weak only because he has depended on help from outside, and who unhesitatingly throws himself on his own thought, instantly rights himself, stands erect, assumes a dominant attitude, and works miracles.

Scientists tell us that we live in the universal ether. This is formless of itself, but it is pliable and forms about us, in us, and around us, according to our thought and word. We set it into activity by that which we think. Then that which manifests to us objectively is that which we have thought or said.

Thought is governed by law. The reason we have not manifested more faith is because of lack of understanding. We have not understood that everything works in exact accordance with definite law. The law of thought is as definite as the laws of mathematics, or the laws of chemistry, or the laws of electricity, or the law of gravitation. When we begin to understand that happiness, health, success, prosperity, and every other condition or environment are results and that these results are created by right thinking, either consciously or unconsciously, we shall realize the importance of a working knowledge of the laws governing thought.

Those coming into a conscious realization of the power of thought find themselves in possession of the best that life can give. Substantial things of a higher order become theirs and these sublime realities are so constituted that they can be made tangible parts of daily personal life. They realize a world of higher power and keep that power constantly working. This power is inexhaustible, limitless, and they are therefore carried forward from victory to victory. Obstacles that seem insurmountable are overcome. Enemies are changed to friends, conditions are overcome, elements transformed, and fate is conquered.

The supply of good is inexhaustible and the demand can be made along whatever lines we may desire. This is the mental law of demand and supply.

Our circumstances and environment are formed by our thoughts. We have, perhaps, been creating these conditions unconsciously. If they are unsatisfactory, the remedy is to consciously alter our mental attitude and see out circumstances adjust themselves to the new mental condition. There is nothing strange or supernatural about this. It is simply the Law of Being. The thoughts which take root in the mind will certainly produce fruit after their kind. The greatest schemer cannot "gather grapes of thorns, or figs of thistles." To improve our conditions, we must first improve ourselves. Our thoughts and desires will be the first to show improvement.

To be in ignorance of the laws governing in the mental world is to be like a child playing with fire or a man manipulating powerful chemicals without a knowledge of their nature and relations. This is universally true because Mind is the one great cause that produces all conditions in the lives of men and women.

Admitting that you agree with everything that has been stated thus far (and most persons will take no exception to anything that has been said), it still remains to make a practical application of the law.

In order to take advantage of this law and put ourselves into harmonious relationship with it so that the benefit may be made manifest in our lives, it is necessary to see that the conditions are all met for its proper operation. We may know the laws governing electricity, we may have all the proper mechanisms (the lights, the globes, the wires, the buttons), and we may even know how to generate the power, but if the connections are not properly made, we can push the button until doomsday and no light will appear. So with the Law of Attraction. It is in operation all the time, everywhere. Something is constantly being created, something is appearing, everything is continually changing. But to take advantage of this process, it is just as necessary to comply with the law as it is in the case of electricity or gravitation.

Mind is creative and operates through the Law of Attraction. We are not to try to influence any to do what we think they should do. Each individual has a right to choose for himself, but aside from this we would be operating under the laws of force, which are destructive in their nature and just the opposite of the Law of Attraction. A little reflection will convince you that all of the great laws of nature operate in silence and that the underlying principle is the Law of Attraction. It is only destructive processes such as earthquakes and catastrophes that employ force. Nothing good is ever accomplished in that way.

To be successful, attention must invariably be directed to the creative plane–it must never be competitive. You do not wish to take anything away from any one else. You want to create something for yourself, and what you want for yourself you are perfectly willing that everyone else should have.

You know that it is not necessary to take from one to give to another, but that the supply for all is abundant. Nature's storehouse of wealth is inexhaustible and if there seems to be a lack of supply anywhere, it is only because the channels of distribution are as yet imperfect.

Abundance is a natural law of the universe. The evidence of this law is conclusive. We see it on every hand. Everywhere nature is lavish, wasteful, and extravagant. Nowhere is economy observed in any created thing. Profusion is manifested in everything. The millions and millions of trees and flowers and plants and animals and the vast scheme of reproduction where the process of creating and recreating is forever going on all indicates the lavishness with which Nature has made provision for man. That there is an abundance for everyone is evident, but that many seem to have been separated from this supply is also evident–they have not yet come into a realization of the Universality of all substance and that mind is the active principle that starts causes in motion whereby we are related to the things we desire.

It is evident, therefore, that he who fails to fully investigate and take advantage of the wonderful progress that is being made in this last and greatest science, will soon be as far behind as the man who would refuse to acknowledge and accept the benefits which have accrued to mankind through an understanding of the laws of electricity.

Of course, mind creates negative conditions just as readily as favourable conditions, and when we consciously or unconsciously visualize every kind of lack, limitation, and discord, we create these conditions. This is what many are unconsciously doing all the time.

This law, as well as every other law, is no respecter of persons, but it is in constant operation and is relentlessly bringing to each individual exactly what he has created. In other words, "Whatsoever a man soweth that shall he also reap."

Abundance, therefore, depends upon a recognition of the Laws of Abundance, and the fact that Mind is not only the creator, but the only creator of all there is. Certainly nothing can be created, before we know that it can be created and then make the proper effort. There is no more electricity in the world today than there was fifty years ago, but until someone recognized the law by which it could be made of service, we received no benefit. Now that the law is understood, practically the whole world is lit by it. So with the Law of Abundance: It is only those who recognize the law and place themselves in harmony with it, who share in its benefits.

A recognition of the Law of Abundance develops certain mental and moral qualities, among which are Courage, Loyalty, Tact, Sagacity, Individuality, and Constructiveness. These are all modes of thought. And as all thought is creative, they manifest in objective conditions corresponding with the mental condition. This is necessarily true because the ability of the individual to think is his ability to act upon the Universal Mind and bring it into manifestation. It is the process whereby the individual becomes a channel for the differentiation of the Universal. Every thought is a cause and every condition an effect.

This principle endows the individual with seemingly transcendental possibilities, among which is the mastery of conditions through the creation and recognition of opportunities. This creation of opportunity implies the existence or creation of the necessary qualities or talents that are thought forces and which result in a consciousness of power that future events cannot disturb. It is this organization of victory or success within the mind, this consciousness of power within which constitutes the responsive harmonious action whereby we are related to the objects and purposes that we seek. This is the Law of Attraction in action. This Law, being the common property of all, can be exercised by any one having sufficient knowledge of its operation.

Courage is that power of the mind that manifests in the love of mental conflict. It is a noble and lofty sentiment. It is equally fitted to command or obey. Both require courage. It often has a tendency to conceal itself. There are men and women, too, who apparently exist only to do what is pleasing to others, but when the time comes and the latent will is revealed, we find under the velvet glove an iron hand–and no mistake about it. True courage is cool, calm, and collected, and is never fool-hardy, quarrelsome, ill-natured, or contentious.

Accumulation is the power to reserve and preserve a part of the supply that we are constantly receiving so as to be in position to take advantage of the larger opportunities that will come as soon as we are ready for them. Has it not been said, "To him that hath shall be given." All successful business men have this quality well-developed. James J. Hill, who died leaving an estate of over fifty-two million dollars, said, "If you want to know whether you are destined to be a success or a failure in life, you can easily find out. The test is simple and it is infallible: Are you able to save money? If not, drop out. You will lose. You may think not, but you will lose as sure as you live. The seed of success is not in you." This is very good so far as it goes, but any one who knows the biography of James J. Hill knows that he acquired his fifty million dollars by following the exact methods we have given. In the first place, he started with nothing–he had to use his imagination to idealize the vast railroad which he projected across the western prairies. He then had to come into a recognition of the Law of Abundance in order to provide the ways and means for materializing it. Unless he had followed out this program, he would never have had anything to save.

Accumulativeness acquires momentum. The more you accumulate the more you desire and the more you desire the more you accumulate, so that it is but a short time until the action and reaction acquire a momentum that cannot be stopped. It must, however, never be confounded with selfishness, miserliness, or penuriousness. They are perversions and will make any true progress impossible.

Constructiveness is the creative instinct of the mind. It will be readily seen that every successful business man must be able to plan, develop, or construct. In the business world, it is usually referred to as initiative. It is not enough to go along in the beaten path. New ideas must be developed as well as new ways of doing things. It manifests in building, designing, planning, inventing, discovering, improving. It is a most valuable quality and must be constantly encouraged and developed. Every individual possesses it in some degree because he is a center of consciousness in that Infinite and Eternal Energy from which all things proceed.

Water manifests on three planes: As ice, as water, and as steam. It is all the same compound, the only difference is the temperature, but no one would try to drive an engine with ice. Convert it to steam and it easily takes up the load. So with your energy: If you want it to act on the creative plane, you will have to begin by melting the ice with the fire of imagination and you will find that the stronger the fire and the more ice you melt, the more powerful your thought will become and the easier it will be for you to materialize your desire.

Sagacity is the ability to perceive and cooperate with Natural Law. True Sagacity avoids trickery and deceit as it would the leprosy. It is the product of that deep insight that enables one to penetrate into the heart of things and understand how to set causes in motion that will inevitably create successful conditions.

Tact is a very subtle—and at the same time a very important factor—in business success. It is very similar to intuition. To possess tact, one must have a fine feeling and must instinctively know what to say or what to do. In order to be tactful, one must possess Sympathy and Understanding—that understanding which is so rare, for all men see and hear and feel, but how desperately few "understand." Tact enables one to foresee what is about to happen and calculate the result of actions. Tact enables us to feel when we are in the presence of physical, mental, and moral cleanliness, for these are today invariably demanded as the price of success.

Loyalty is one of the strongest links that bind men of strength and character. It is one that can never be broken with impunity. The man who would lose his right hand rather than betray a friend will never lack friends. The man who will stand in silent guard until death, if need be, beside the shrine of confidence or friendship of those who have allowed him to enter will find himself linked with a current of cosmic power which will attract desirable conditions only. It is inconceivable that such a one should ever meet with lack of any kind.

Individuality is the power to unfold our own latent possibilities, to be a law unto ourselves, to be interested in the race rather than the goal. Strong men care nothing for the flock of imitators who trot complacently behind them. They derive no satisfaction in the mere leading of large numbers or the plaudits of the mob. This pleases only petty natures and inferior minds. Individuality glories more in the unfolding of the power within than in the servility of the weakling.

Individuality is a real power inherent in all and the development and consequent expression of this power enables one to assume the responsibility of directing his own footsteps rather than stampeding after some self-assertive bell-weather.

Truth is the imperative condition of all well-being. To be sure, to know the truth and to stand confidently on it is a satisfaction beside which no other is comparable. Truth is the underlying verity, the condition precedent to every business or social relation. Truth is the only solid ground in a world of conflict, doubt, and danger.

Every act not in harmony with Truth, whether through ignorance or design, cuts the ground from under our feet, leads to discord and inevitable loss and confusion. For while the humblest mind can accurately foretell the result of every correct action, the greatest and most profound and penetrating mind loses its way hopelessly and can form no conception of the results due to a departure from correct principles.

Those who establish within themselves the requisite elements of true success have established confidence, organized victory, and it only remains for them to take such steps from time to time as the newly-awakened thought force will direct. And herein rests the magical secret of all power.

Less than ten percent of our mental process is conscious. The other ninety percent is subconscious and unconscious, so that he who would depend upon his conscious thought alone for results is less than ten percent efficient. Those who are accomplishing anything worth while are those who are enabled to take advantage of this greater storehouse of mental wealth. It is in the vast domain of the subconscious mind that great truths are hidden and it is here that thought finds its creative power, its power to correlate with its object, to bring out of the unseen the seen.

Those familiar with the laws of electricity understand the principle that electricity must always pass from a higher to a lower potentiality and can therefore make whatever application of the power they desire. Those not familiar with this law can effect nothing. And so with the laws governing the Mental World. Those who understand that Mind penetrates all things, is Omnipresent, and is responsive to every demand, can make use of the law and can control conditions, circumstances, and environment. The uninformed cannot use it because they do not know it.

The fruit of this knowledge is, as it were, a gift of the Gods. It is the "truth" that makes men free. Not only free from every lack and limitation, but free from sorrow, worry, and care. Is it not wonderful to realize that this law is no respecter of persons? That it makes no difference what your habit of thought may be? The way has been prepared.

With the realization that this mental power controls and

directs every other power that exists, that it can be cultivated and developed, that no limitation can be placed upon its activity, it will become apparent that it is the greatest fact in the world, the remedy for every ill, the solution for every difficulty, the gratification of every desire. In fact, that it is the Creator's magnificent provision for human emancipation.

The Master Key System

The Master Key System is concerned with causes rather than effects, demonstration rather than theory, the practical rather than the abstract.

It is rapidly growing in favour by reason of its great simplicity and because it furnishes an explanation for many hitherto unknown facts and a conceivable explanation for many more.

It is a force which is gaining momentum with a rapidity and certainty that is the despair of the defenders of tradition and reaction.

This is largely true because it avoids theory, speculation, and abstractions of all kinds, and confines itself to the operation of natural laws.

These laws operate with scientific exactitude and those who have succeeded in obtaining a working knowledge of them are enabled to break the bonds of environment, control elementary forces, and utilize the potentialities of Infinity.

For many years little or nothing was permitted to be revealed to the general public concerning the esoteric teachings, but within the last twenty-five years there has been greater freedom in this respect. Until now, they form an important part of nearly all teachings where ultimate truth is an objective.

Vaguely, throughout the world, the idea has been diffused that there was some process of study that men here and there did follow and which led to the acquisition of a higher kind of knowledge than that taught in books or by public teachers.

But it was invariably found that this knowledge was jealously guarded and the student was bound to the most inviolable secrecy as to everything connected with his progress, so that it was impossible to imagine anything more improbable than the unauthorized revelation of such information by any student of the great schools of esoteric philosophy.

This was true because those in authority were afraid of the result of premature disclosure of these important principles. They feared that an unprepared public mind might not be ready to make proper use of the extraordinary power that the application of these principles disclosed.

But the approaches to scientific understanding are open to all and persistent study has revealed hidden passages which lead to the grandest imaginable realms of enlightenment.

For a time it was possible to delude the general public with the idea that transmutation was on the plane of matter alone and they continued to remain in ignorance of the fact that this was but a correspondence and that the higher forms of alchemy takes place in Mental and Spiritual realms.

It is in these realms that the practical art of manipulating the forces of Nature was discovered and the application of this knowledge to matters of daily life invests the student with such extraordinary power that the results seem altogether miraculous.

Many have sensed the principles taught in The Master Key System, but in their reaction from materialistic bondage they have taken one-sided views and have followed mental and spiritual ideas without a due recognition of the importance of natural laws and have become impractical idealists. A denial of the truth is not a factor in progress.

The Master Key System will enable you to discern things as they are rather than as they seem.

The scientific spirit now dominates every field of effort. Relations of cause and effect are no longer ignored.

The discovery of a reign of law marked an epoch in human progress. It eliminated the element of uncertainty and caprice from mens' lives and substituted law, reason, and certitude.

Men now understand that for every result there is an adequate and definite cause, so that when a given result is desired, they seek the condition by which alone this result may be attained.

The basis upon which all law rests was discovered by inductive reasoning, which consists of comparing a number of separate instances with one another until the common factor that gives rise to them all is seen.

It is this method of study to which the civilized nations owe the greater part of their prosperity and the more valuable part of their knowledge. It has lengthened life. It has mitigated pain. It has spanned rivers. It has brightened night with the splendour of day. It extended the range of vision, accelerated motion, annihilated distance, facilitated intercourse, and enabled men to descend into the sea and to soar in the air. What wonder then that men soon endeavoured to extend the blessings of this system of study to their method of thinking, so that when it became plainly evident that certain results followed a particular method of thinking it only remained to classify these results.

This method is scientific and it is the only method by which we shall be permitted to retain that degree of liberty and freedom that we have been accustomed to look upon as an inalienable right because as Prof. A.F. Lange, director of the California University School of Education, says, "Democracy is safe at home and in the world only if national preparedness means such things as growing surplus of health, accumulated efficiency in public and private business of whatever sort, continuous advance in the science and art of acting together, and the increasingly dominant endeavour to make all of these and all other aspects of national development center and revolve about ascending life, single and collective, for which science, art, and ethics furnish guidance and controlling motives."

The Master Key System is based on absolute scientific truth and will unfold the possibilities that lie dormant in the individual and teach how they may be brought into powerful action to increase the person's effective capacity, bringing added energy, discernment, vigour, and mental elasticity. The student who gains an understanding of the mental laws that are unfolded will come into the possession of an ability to secure results hitherto undreamed of and which has rewards hardly to be expressed in words.

It explains the correct use of both the receptive and active elements of the mental nature and instructs the student in the recognition of opportunity. It strengthens the will and reasoning powers and teaches the cultivation and best uses of imagination, desire, the emotions, and the intuitional faculty. It gives initiative, tenacity of purpose, wisdom of choice, intelligent sympathy, and a thorough enjoyment of life on its higher planes.

The Master Key System teaches the use of Mind Power—true Mind Power—not any of the substitutes and perversions. It has nothing to do with Hypnotism, Magic, or any of the more or less fascinating deceptions by which many are led to think that something can be had for nothing.

The Master Key System cultivates and develops the understanding that will enable you to control the body and thereby the health. It improves and strengthens the Memory. It develops Insight, the kind of Insight that is so rare, the kind that is the distinguishing characteristic of every successful business man, the kind that enables men to see the possibilities as well as the difficulties in every situation, the kind that enables men to discern opportunity close at hand for thousands fail to see opportunities almost within their grasp while they are industriously working with situations which under no possibility can be made to realize any substantial return.

The Master Key System develops Mental Power, which means that others will instinctively recognize that you are a person of force, of character—that they will want to do what you want them to do. It means that you will attract men and things to you and that you will be what some people call "lucky" and that "things" will come your way. It means that you have come into an understanding of the fundamental laws of Nature and have put yourself in harmony with them, that you are in tune with the Infinite, that you understand the Law of Attraction, the Natural laws of growth, and the Psychological laws on which all advantages in the social and business world rest.

Mental Power is creative power. It gives you the ability to create for yourself. It does not mean the ability to take something away from some one else. Nature never does things that way. Nature makes two blades of grass grow where one grew before and Mind Power enables men to do the same thing.

The Master Key System develops insight and sagacity, increased independence, the ability and disposition to be helpful; it destroys distrust, depression, fear, melancholia, and every form of lack, limitation, and weakness, including pain and disease; it awakens buried talents, supplies initiative, force, energy, vitality. It awakens an appreciation of the beautiful in Art, Literature, and Science.

It has changed the lives of thousands of men and women by substituting definite principles for uncertain and hazy methods—and principles are the foundation upon which every system of efficiency must rest.

The president of the largest corporation in the United States [Elbert Gary of the United States Steel Corporation] once said, "The services of advisors, instructors, efficiency experts in successful management are indispensable to most business enterprises of magnitude, but I deem the recognition and adoption of right principles of vastly more importance." The Master Key System teaches right principles and suggests methods for making a practical application of the principles. In that it differs from every other course of study, it teaches that the only possible value that can attach to any principle is in its application. Many read books, take home study courses, attend lectures all their lives without ever making any progress in demonstrating the value of the principles involved. The Master Key System suggests methods by which the value of the principles taught may be demonstrated and put in actual practice in the daily experience.

There is a change in the thought of the world. This change is silently transpiring in our midst and is more important than any which the world has undergone since the downfall of Paganism.

The present revolution in the opinions of all classes of men, the highest and most cultured of men as well as those of the labouring class, stands unparalleled in the history of the world.

Science has of late made such vast discoveries, has revealed such an infinity of resources, has unveiled such enormous possibilities and such unsuspected forces, that scientific men more and more hesitate to affirm certain theories as established and indubitable or to deny certain other theories as absurd or impossible. And so a new civilization is being born. Customs, creeds, and cruelty are passing; vision, faith, and service are taking their place. The fetters of tradition are being melted off from humanity, and as the dross of materialism is being consumed, thought is being liberated and truth is rising full orbed before an astonished multitude.

The whole world is on the eve of a new consciousness, a new power, and a new realization of the resources within the self. The last century saw the most magnificent material progress in history. The new century will produce the greatest progress in mental and spiritual power.

Physical Science has resolved matter into molecules, molecules into atoms, atoms into energy, and it has remained for Mr. J. A. Fleming, in an address before the Royal Institution, to resolve this energy into mind. He says, "In its ultimate essence, energy may be incomprehensible by us except as an exhibition of the direct operation of that which we call Mind or Will."

Let us see what are the most powerful forces in Nature. In the mineral world everything is solid and fixed. In the animal and vegetable kingdom it is in a state of flux, forever changing, always being created and recreated. In the atmosphere we find heat, light, and energy. Each realm becomes finer and more spiritual as we pass from the visible to the invisible, from the coarse to the fine, from the low potentiality to high potentiality. When we reach the invisible we find energy in its purest and most volatile state.

And as the most powerful forces of Nature are the invisible forces, so we find that the most powerful forces of man are his invisible forces—his spiritual force—and the only way in which the spiritual force can manifest is through the process of thinking. Thinking is the only activity that the spirit possesses and thought is the only product of thinking.

Addition and subtraction are therefore spiritual transactions. Reasoning is a spiritual process. Ideas are spiritual conceptions. Questions are spiritual searchlights. Logic, argument, and philosophy are spiritual machinery.

Every thought brings into action certain physical tissue, parts of the brain, nerve of muscle. This produces an actual physical change in the construction of the tissue. Therefore it is only necessary to have a certain number of thoughts on a given subject in order to bring about a complete change in the physical organization of a man.

This is the process by which failure is changed to success. Thoughts of courage, power, inspiration, and harmony are substituted for thoughts of failure, despair, lack, limitation, and discord. And as these thoughts take root, the physical tissue is changed and the individual sees life is a new light. Old things have actually passed away, all things have become new. He is born again, this time born of the spirit and life has a new meaning for him. He is reconstructed and is filled with joy, confidence, hope, and energy. He sees opportunities for success to which he was heretofore blind. He recognizes possibilities which before had no meaning for him. The thoughts of success with which he has been impregnated are radiated to those around him and they in turn help him onward and upward. He attracts to him new and successful associates and this in turn changes his environment, so that by this simple exercise of thought, a man changes not only himself, but his environment, circumstances, and conditions.

You will see—you must see!—that we are at the dawn of a

new day. That the possibilities are so wonderful, so fascinating, so limitless as to be almost bewildering. A century ago, any man with an aeroplane or even a Gatling gun could have annihilated a whole army equipped with the implements of warfare then in use. So it is at present. Any man with a knowledge of the possibilities contained in the Master Key has an inconceivable advantage over the multitude.

The Master Key System comes in twenty-four parts, one part is mailed each week. Each part has a series of questions by which your understanding of the lesson is tested. You are invited and urged to ask any and all questions that may occur to you concerning the lesson or the application of the principles in question to your own particular problem.

Many have found this privilege worth many times the cost of the entire service. Many have stated that the advice received in this way was invaluable.

Review of The Master Key

Doctor T. R. Sanjivi
Editor of
The Kalpaka
Tinnevelly, S. India

Review of The Master Key

This is an age of enquiry and ergo of discovery. And the greatest discovery of the age is the discovery of the Thought-Force or Thought-Power. Its importance, however, has not as yet penetrated human consciousness as it is believed to have in the brilliant days of India's renown, at least in the cultured circles.

The system under review is truly a clear presentation of the creative power of correct thinking and has been carefully and scientifically prepared so that students may prove for themselves the importance of the practical results to be derived from a regular course of instruction.

This course consists of twenty-four parts. Part One deals with the relations between the world within and the world without. Part Two deals with the two modes of mental activity and contains directions for impressing the subconscious. "How to awake the solar plexus and completely eliminate fear" is dealt with in Part Three. Among other things, Part Four speaks of the development of faith and courage and Part Five the secret of concentration, visualization, and the materialization of ideals. The next three parts are important as they contain splendid instructions for the cultivation of imagination, the secret of the solution to every problem, and a good sadhana demonstrating the Law of Abundance. Other Parts continue the useful hints and instructions concerning the dynamic power of thought, of mental harmony and efficiency, the mastery of fate or Karma, the law whereby the sadhaka may control other forms of intelligence, the elimination of sickness, an the secret of mental therapeutics. Part Twenty-three is a solace to those who are ignorant of the practical nature of spirituality. The last Part is by no means the least useful and is a blessing to those who desire to master the marvelous secrets of the theory and practice of constructive thinking. This is the final lesson that exhorts the student to know truth. By studying these several lessons, the student will know that he is a wonderful being with wonderful latent forces and resources in a truly wonderful Universe. The students who are ambitious will enjoy this course. Many of the methods suggested or described herein may be of assistance to him in his struggle for existence.

The roof and crown of these valuable instructions is of course that portion relating to the exercises for visualization and concentration by which we may secure control of the priceless machinery of the Mind. In conclusion, we wish to say we have enjoyed the course and would advise those interested to study inwardly, digest, and profit by the instructions.

"Entering into the Spirit of It" & "Individuality"

from

The Dore Lectures on Mental Science (1909)

Thomas Troward

Thomas Troward
(1847-1916)

Thomas Troward was born in Punjab, India, in 1847 to Albany and Frederica Troward. He was brought back to England to attend school and in 1865, at the age of 18, he graduated from college with gold medal honours in literature.

At age 22, in 1869, he returned to India and took the difficult Indian Civil Service Examination. One of the subjects was metaphysics and Troward surprised everyone with his answers because of their originality. He became an assistant commissioner and was quickly promoted to Divisional Judge in the Punjab, where he served for the next 25 years. In India, he married his first wife. Together, they had three children. He married a second time after his first wife died and had three more children. His second wife, Sarah Ann, helped in the publishing of his works after his death.

People described him as a kind and understanding man, simple and natural in manner. While in India, he learned the language of the country. He studied all of the bibles of the world, including the Koran, Hindu scriptures, and books of Raja Yoga. His studies in original Hebrew provided the foundation for his book, Bible Mystery and Bible Meaning.

Troward's genius did not go unrecognized. The philosopher William James characterized Troward's Edinburgh Lectures on Mental Science as "far and away the ablest statement of philosophy I have met, beautiful in its sustained clearness of thought and style, a really classic statement."

Thomas Troward died on May 16, 1916, at the age of 69.

The Dore Lectures on Mental Science

Entering into the Spirit of It

We all know the meaning of this phrase in our everyday life. The Spirit is that which gives life and movement to anything, in fact it is that which causes it to exist at all. The thought of the author, the impression of the painter, the feeling of the musician, is that without which their works could never have come into being, and so it is only as we enter into the idea which gives rise to the work, that we can derive all the enjoyment and benefit from it which it is able to bestow. If we cannot enter into the Spirit of it, the book, the picture, the music, are meaningless to us: to appreciate them we must share the mental attitude of their creator. This is a universal principle; if we do not enter into the Spirit of a thing, it is dead so far as we are concerned; but if we do enter into it we reproduce in ourselves the same quality of life which called that thing into existence.

Now if this is a general principle, why can we not carry it to a higher range of things? Why not to the highest point of all? May we not enter into the originating Spirit of Life itself, and so reproduce it in ourselves as a perennial spring of livingness?

This, surely, is a question worthy of our careful consideration.

The spirit of a thing is that which is the source of its inherent movement, and therefore the question before us is, what is the nature of the primal moving power, which is at the back of the endless array of life which we see around us, our own life included? Science gives us ample ground for saying that it is not material, for science has now, at least theoretically, reduced all material things to a primary ether, universally distributed, whose innumerable particles are in absolute equilibrium; whence it follows on mathematical grounds alone that the initial movement which began to concentrate the world and all material substances out of the particles of the dispersed ether, could not have originated in the particles themselves. Thus by a necessary deduction from the conclusions of physical science, we are compelled to realize the presence of some immaterial power capable of separating off certain specific areas for the display of cosmic activity, and then building up a material universe with all its inhabitants by an orderly sequence of evolution, in which each stage lays the foundation for the development of the stage, which is to follow—in a word we find ourselves brought face to face with a power which exhibits on a stupendous scale, the faculties of selection and adaptation of means to ends, and thus distributes energy and life in accordance with a recognizable scheme of cosmic progression. It is therefore not only Life, but also Intelligence, and Life guided by Intelligence becomes Volition. It is this primary originating power which we mean when we speak of "The Spirit," and it is into this Spirit of the whole universe that we must enter if we would reproduce it as a spring of Original Life in ourselves.

Now in the case of the productions of artistic genius we know that we must enter into the movement of the creative mind of the artist, before we can realize the principle which gives rise to his work. We must learn to partake of the feeling, to find expression for which is the motive of his creative activity. May we not apply the same principle to the Greater Creative Mind with which we are seeking to deal? There is something in the work of the artist which is akin to that of original creation. His work—literary, musical, or graphic—is original creation on a miniature scale, and in this it differs from that of the engineer, which is constructive, or that of the scientist which is analytical; for the artist in a sense creates something out of nothing, and therefore starts from the stand-point of simple feeling, and not from that of a pre-existing necessity. This, by the hypothesis of the case, is true also of the Parent Mind, for at the stage where the initial movement of creation takes place, there are no existing conditions to compel action in one direction more than another. Consequently the direction taken by the creative impulse is not dictated by outward circumstances, and the primary movement must therefore be entirely due to the action of the Original Mind upon itself; it is the reaching out of this Mind for realization of all that it feels itself to be.

The creative process thus in the first instance is purely a matter of feeling—exactly what we speak of as "motif" in a work of art.

Now it is this original feeling that we need to enter into, because it is the "fons et origo" of the whole chain of causation which subsequently follows. What then can this original feeling of the Spirit be? Since the Spirit is "Life in itself," its feeling can only be for the fuller expression of Life—any other sort of feeling would be self-destructive and is therefore inconceivable.

Then the full expression of Life implies Happiness, and Happiness implies Harmony, and Harmony implies Order, and Order implies Proportion, and Proportion implies Beauty; so that in recognizing the inherent tendency of the Spirit towards the production of Life, we can recognize a similar inherent tendency to the production of these other qualities also; and since the desire to bestow the greater fullness of joyous life can only be described as Love, we can sum up the whole of the feeling which is the original moving impulse in the Spirit as Love and Beauty—the Spirit finding expression through forms of beauty in centres of life, in harmonious reciprocal relation to itself. This is a generalized statement of the broad principle by which Spirit expands from the innermost to the outermost, in accordance with a Law of tendency inherent in itself.

It sees itself, as it were, reflected in various centres of life and energy, each with its appropriate form; but in the first instance these reflections can have no existence except within the originating Mind. They have their first beginning as mental images, so that in addition to the powers of Intelligence and Selection, we must also realize that of Imagination as belonging to the Divine Mind; and we must picture these powers as working from the initial motive of Love and Beauty.

Now this is the Spirit that we need to enter into, and the method of doing so is a perfectly logical one. It is the same method by which all scientific advance is made. It consists in first observing how a certain law works under the conditions spontaneously provided by nature, next in carefully considering what principle this spontaneous working indicates, and lastly deducing from this how the same principle would act under specially selected conditions, not spontaneously provided by nature.

The progress of shipbuilding affords a good example of what I mean. Formerly wood was employed instead of iron, because wood floats in water and iron sinks; yet now the navies of the world are built of iron; careful thought showed the law of flotation to be that anything could float which, bulk for bulk, is lighter than the mass of liquid displaced by it; and so we now make iron float by the very same law by which it sinks, because by the introduction of the personal factor, we provide conditions which do not occur spontaneously–according to the esoteric maxim that "Nature unaided fails." Now we want to apply the same process of specializing a generic Law to the first of all Laws, that of the generic life-giving tendency of Spirit itself. Without the element of individual personality the Spirit can only work cosmically by a generic Law; but this law admits of far higher specialization, and this specialization can only be attained through the introduction of the personal factor. But to introduce this factor the individual must be fully aware of the principle which underlies the spontaneous or cosmic action of the law.

Where, then, will he find this principle of Life? Certainly not by contemplating Death. In order to get a principle to work in the way we require it to, we must observe its action when it is working spontaneously in this particular direction. We must ask why it goes in the right direction as far as it does–and having learnt this we shall then be able to make it go further. The law of flotation was not discovered by contemplating the sinking of things, but by contemplating the floating of things which floated naturally, and then intelligently asking why they did so.

The knowledge of a principle is to be gained by the study of its affirmative action; when we understand that we are in a position to correct the negative conditions which tend to prevent that action.

Now Death is the absence of Life, and disease is the absence of health, so to enter into the Spirit of Life we require to contemplate it, where it is to be found, and not where it is not—we are met with the old question, "Why seek ye the living among the dead?" This is why we start our studies by considering the cosmic creation, for it is there that we find the Life Spirit working through untold ages, not merely as deathless energy, but with a perpetual advance into higher degrees of Life. If we could only so enter into the Spirit as to make it personally in ourselves what it evidently is in itself, the magnum opus would be accomplished. This means realizing our life as drawn direct from the Originating Spirit; and if we now understand that the Thought or Imagination of the Spirit is the great reality of Being, and that all material facts are only correspondences, then it logically follows that what we have to do is to maintain our individual place in the Thought of the Parent Mind.

We have seen that the action of the Originating Mind must needs be generic, that is according to types which include multitudes of individuals. This type is the reflection of the Creative Mind at the level of that particular genius; and at the human level it is Man, not as associated with particular circumstances, but as existing in the absolute ideal.

In proportion then as we learn to dissociate our conception of ourselves from particular circumstances, and to rest upon our absolute nature, as reflections of the Divine ideal, we, in our turn, reflect back into the Divine Imagination its original conception of itself as expressed in generic or typical Man, and so by a natural law of cause and effect, the individual who realizes this mental attitude enters permanently into the Spirit of Life, and it becomes a perennial fountain of Life springing up spontaneously within him.

He then finds himself to be as the Bible says, "the image and likeness of God." He has reached the level at which he affords a new starting point for the creative process, and the Spirit, finding a personal centre in him, begins its work de nova, having thus solved the great problem of how to enable the Universal to act directly upon the plane of the Particular.

It is in this sense, as affording the requisite centre for a new departure of the creative Spirit, that man is said to be a "microcosm," or universe in miniature; and this is also what is meant by the esoteric doctrine of the Octave, of which I may be able to speak more fully on some other occasion.

If the principles here stated are carefully considered, they will be found to throw light on much that would otherwise be obscure, and they will also afford the key to the succeeding essays.

The reader is therefore asked to think them out carefully for himself, and to note their connection with the subject of the next article.

Individuality

Individuality is the necessary complement of the Universal Spirit, which was the subject of our consideration last Sunday. The whole problem of life consists in finding the true relation of the individual to the Universal Originating Spirit; and the first step towards ascertaining this is to realize what the Universal Spirit must be in itself. We have already done this to some extent, and the conclusions we have arrived at are:

That the essence of the Spirit is Life, Love, and Beauty.

That its Motive, or primary moving impulse, is to express the Life, Love and Beauty which it feels itself to be.

That the Universal cannot act on the plane of the Particular except by becoming the particular, that is by expression through the individual.

If these three axioms are clearly grasped, we have got a solid foundation from which to start our consideration of the subject for today.

The first question that naturally presents itself is,

If these things be so, why does not every individual express the life, love, and beauty of the Universal Spirit?

The answer to this question is to be found in the Law of Consciousness. We cannot be conscious of anything except by realizing a certain relation between it and ourselves. It must affect us in some way, otherwise we are not conscious of its existence; and according to the way in which it affects us we recognize ourselves as standing related to it. It is this self-recognition on our own part carried out to the sum total of all our relations, whether spiritual, intellectual, or physical, that constitutes our realization of life. On this principle, then, for the realization of its own Livingness, the production of centres of life, through its relation to which this conscious realization can be attained, becomes a necessity for the Originating Mind. Then it follows that this realization can only be complete where the individual has perfect liberty to withhold it; for otherwise no true realization could have taken place. For instance, let us consider the working of Love. Love must be spontaneous, or it has no existence at all. We cannot imagine such a thing as mechanically induced love. But anything which is formed so as to automatically produce an effect without any volition of its own, is nothing but a piece of mechanism. Hence if the Originating Mind is to realize the reality of Love, it can only be by relation to some being which has the power to withhold love. The same applies to the realization of all the other modes of livingness; so that it is only in proportion, as the individual life is an independent centre of action, with the option of acting either positively or negatively, that any real life has been produced at all. The further the created thing is from being a merely mechanical arrangement, the higher is the grade of creation. The solar system is a perfect work of mechanical creation, but to constitute centres which can reciprocate the highest nature of the Divine Mind, requires not a mechanism, however perfect, but a mental centre which is, in itself, an independent source of action. Hence by the requirements of the case man should be capable of placing himself either in a positive or a negative relation to the Parent Mind, from which he originates; otherwise he would be nothing more than a clockwork figure.

In this necessity of the case, then, we find the reason why the life, love, and beauty of the Spirit are not visibly reproduced in every human being. They are reproduced in the world of nature, so far as a mechanical and automatic action can represent them, but their perfect reproduction can only take place on the basis of a liberty akin to that of the Originating Spirit itself, which therefore implies the liberty of negation as well as of affirmation.

Why, then, does the individual make a negative choice? Because he does not understand the law of his own individuality, and believes it to be a law of limitation, instead of a Law of Liberty. He does not expect to find the starting point of the Creative Process reproduced within himself, and so he looks to the mechanical side of things for the basis of his reasoning about life. Consequently his reasoning lands him in the conclusion that life is limited, because he has assumed limitation in his premises, and so logically cannot escape from it in his conclusion. Then he thinks that this is the law and so ridicules the idea of transcending it. He points to the sequence of cause and effect, by which death, disease, and disaster, hold their sway over the individual, and says that sequence is law.

And he is perfectly right so far as he goes–it is a law; but not the Law. When we have only reached this stage of comprehension, we have yet to learn that a higher law can include a lower one so completely as entirely to swallow it up.

The fallacy involved in this negative argument is the assumption that the law of limitation is essential in all grades of being. It is the fallacy of the old shipbuilders as to the impossibility of building iron ships. What is required is to get at the principle which is at the back of the Law in its affirmative working, and specialize it under higher conditions than are spontaneously presented by nature, and this can only be done by the introduction of the personal element, that is to say an individual intelligence capable of comprehending the principle.

The question, then, is, What is the principle by which we came into being? and this is only a personal application of the general question, How did anything come into being? Now, as I pointed out in the preceding article, the ultimate deduction from physical science is that the originating movement takes place in the Universal Mind, and is analogous to that of our own imagination; and as we have just seen, the perfect ideal can only be that of a being capable of reciprocating all the qualities of the Originating Mind. Consequently man, in his inmost nature, is the product of the Divine Mind imaging forth an image of itself on the plane of the relative as the complementary to its own sphere of the absolute.

If we will therefore go to the inmost principle in ourselves, which philosophy and Scripture alike declare to be made in the image and likeness of God, instead of to the outer vehicles which it externalizes as instruments through which to function on the various planes of being, we shall find that we have reached a principle in ourselves which stands "in loco dei" towards all our vehicles and also towards our environment. It is above them all, and creates them, however unaware we may be of the fact, and relatively to them it occupies the place of first cause. The recognition of this is the discovery of our own relation to the whole world of the relative. On the other hand this must not lead us into the mistake of supposing that there is nothing higher, for, as we have already seen, this inmost principle or ego is itself the effect of an antecedent cause, for it proceeds from the imaging process in the Divine Mind.

We thus find ourselves holding an intermediate position between true First Cause, on the one hand, and the world of secondary causes on the other, and in order to understand the nature of this position, we must fall back on the axiom that the Universal can only work on the plane of the Particular through the individual. Then we see that the function of the individual is to differentiate the undistributed flow of the Universal into suitable directions for starting different trains of secondary causation.

Man's place in the cosmic order is that of a distributor of the Divine power, subject, however, to the inherent Law of the power which he distributes. We see one instance of this in ordinary science, in the fact that we never create force; all we can do is to distribute it. The very word "Man" means distributor or measurer, as in common with all words derived from the Sanderit root "MN." It implies the idea of measurement, just as in the words moon, month, mens, mind, and "man," the Indian weight of 80 lbs.; and it is for this reason that man is spoken of in Scripture as a "steward," or dispenser of the Divine gifts. As our minds become open to the full meaning of this position, the immense possibilities and also the responsibility contained in it will become apparent.

It means that the individual is the creative centre of his own world. Our past experience affords no evidence against this, but on the contrary, is evidence for it. Our true nature is always present, only we have hitherto taken the lower and mechanical side of things for our starting point, and so have created limitation instead of expansion. And even with the knowledge of the Creative Law which we have now attained, we shall continue to do this, if we seek our starting point in the things which are below us and not in the only thing which is above us, namely the Divine Mind, because it is only there that we can find illimitable Creative Power. Life is being, it is the experience of states of consciousness, and there is an unfailing correspondence between these inner states and our outward conditions. Now we see from the Original Creation that the state of consciousness must be the cause, and the corresponding conditions the effect, because at the starting of the creation no conditions existed, and the working of the Creative Mind upon itself can only have been a state of consciousness. This, then, is clearly the Creative Order—from states to conditions. But we invert this order, and seek to create from conditions to states.

We say, If I had such and such conditions they would produce the state of feeling which I desire; and in so saying we run the risk of making a mistake as to the correspondence, for it may turn out that the particular conditions which we fixed on are not such as would produce the desired state. Or, again, though they might produce it in a certain degree, other conditions might produce it in a still greater degree, while at the same time opening the way to the attainment of still higher states and still better conditions. Therefore our wisest plan is to follow the pattern of the Parent Mind and make mental self-recognition our starting point, knowing that by the inherent Law of Spirit the correlated conditions will come by a natural process of growth. Then the great self-recognition is that of our relation to the Supreme Mind. That is the generating centre and we are distributing centres; just as electricity is generated at the central station and delivered in different forms of power by reason of passing through appropriate centres of distribution, so that in one place it lights a room, in another conveys a message, and in a third drives a tram car. In like manner the power of the Universal Mind takes particular forms through the particular mind of the individual. It does not interfere with the lines of his individuality, but works along them, thus making him, not less, but more himself. It is thus, not a compelling power, but an expanding and illuminating one; so that the more the individual recognizes the reciprocal action between it and himself, the more full of life he must become.

Then also we need not be troubled about future conditions because we know that the All-originating Power is working through us and for us, and that according to the Law proved by the whole existing creation, it produces all the conditions required for the expression of the Life, Love and Beauty which it is, so that we can fully trust it to open the way as we go along. The Great Teacher's words, "Take no thought for the morrow"—and note that the correct translation is "Take no anxious thought"—are the practical application of the soundest philosophy. This does not, of course, mean that we are not to exert ourselves. We must do our share in the work, and not expect God to do for us what He can only do through us. We are to use our common sense and natural faculties in working upon the conditions now present. We must make use of them, as far as they go, but we must not try and go further than the present things require; we must not try to force things, but allow them to grow naturally, knowing that they are doing so under the guidance of the All-Creating Wisdom.

Following this method we shall grow more and more into the habit of looking to mental attitude as the Key to our progress in Life, knowing that everything else must come out of that; and we shall further discover that our mental attitude is eventually determined by the way in which we regard the Divine Mind. Then the final result will be that we shall see the Divine Mind to be nothing else than Life, Love and Beauty—Beauty being identical with Wisdom or the perfect adjustment of parts to whole—and we shall see ourselves to be distributing centres of these primary energies and so in our turn subordinate centres of creative power. And as we advance in this knowledge we shall find that we transcend one law of limitation after another by finding the higher law, of which the lower is but a partial expression, until we shall see clearly before us, as our ultimate goal, nothing less than the Perfect Law of Liberty—not liberty without Law which is anarchy, but Liberty according to Law. In this way we shall find that the Apostle spoke the literal truth when he said that we shall become like Him when we see Him as He is, because the whole process by which our individuality is produced is one of reflection of the image existing in the Divine Mind.

When we thus learn the Law of our own being we shall be able to specialize it in ways of which we have hitherto but little conception, but as in the case of all natural laws the specialization cannot take place until the fundamental principle of the generic law has been fully realized. For these reasons the student should endeavour to realize more and more perfectly, both in theory and practice, the law of the relation between the Universal and the Individual Minds. It is that of reciprocal action. If this fact of reciprocity is grasped, it will be found to explain both why the individual falls short of expressing the fullness of Life, which the Spirit is, and why he can attain to the fullness of that expression; just as the same law explains why iron sinks in water, and how it can be made to float. It is the individualizing of the Universal Spirit, by recognizing its reciprocity to ourselves, that is the secret of the perpetuation and growth of our own individuality.

“Introduction”

from

Natural Law in the Spiritual World

(1890)

Henry Drummond

Henry Drummond
(1851-1897)

Henry Drummond was born in Scotland in 1851. He was a man of varied talents. Perhaps best remembered as a gifted evangelist who assisted Dwight L. Moody during his revival campaigns, he was also a lecturer in natural science.

Although he never received a degree, he was an ordained minister and a professor of theology. He also wrote several books. “Natural Law in the Spiritual World”, published in 1883, sold 70,000 copies in five years and made him famous. He published another popular book, “Tropical Africa”, after making a geological survey of southern Africa. “The Ascent of Man” was also a significant book during his lifetime.

However, “The Greatest Thing in the World”, a meditation he wrote in 1874 that illuminates the importance of Book 1 Verse 13 of Corinthians, is the one that assured he would be remembered by later generations. Widely read and quoted during his lifetime, it went on to sell over 12 million copies and it continues today to influence people to follow God’s two great commandments: to love God and to love each other.

Natural Law in the Spiritual World

Introduction

"This method turns aside from hypotheses not to be tested by any known logical canon familiar to science, whether the hypothesis claims support from intuition, aspiration or general plausibility. And, again, this method turns aside from ideal standards which avow themselves to be lawless, which profess to transcend the field of law. We say, life and conduct will stand for us wholly on a basis of law, and must rest entirely in that region of science (not physical, but moral and social science), where we are free to use our intelligence in the methods known to us as intelligible logic, methods which the intellect can analyse. When you confront us with hypotheses, however sublime and however affecting, if they cannot be stated in terms of the rest of our knowledge, if they are disparate to that world of sequence and sensation which to us is the ultimate base of all our real knowledge, then we shake our heads and turn aside."—Frederick Harrison

"Ethical science is already for ever completed, so far as her general outline and main principles are concerned, and has been, as it were, waiting for physical science to come up with her."—Paradoxical Philosophy

Part I

Natural Law is a new word. It is the last and the most magnificent discovery of science. No more telling proof is open to the modern world of the greatness of the idea than the greatness of the attempts which have always been made to justify it. In the earlier centuries, before the birth of science, Phenomena were studied alone. The world then was a chaos, a collection of single, isolated, and independent facts. Deeper thinkers saw, indeed, that relations must subsist between these facts, but the Reign of Law was never more to the ancients than a far-off vision. Their philosophies, conspicuously those of the Stoics and Pythagoreans, heroically sought to marshal the discrete materials of the universe into thinkable form, but from these artificial and fantastic systems nothing remains to us now but an ancient testimony to the grandeur of that harmony which they failed to reach.

With Copernicus, Galileo, and Kepler the first regular lines of the universe began to be discerned. When Nature yielded to Newton her great secret, Gravitation was felt to be not greater as a fact in itself than as a revelation that Law was fact. And thenceforth the search for individual Phenomena gave way before the larger study of their relations. The pursuit of Law became the passion of science.

What that discovery of Law has done for Nature, it is impossible to estimate. As a mere spectacle the universe to-day discloses a beauty so transcendent that he who disciplines himself by scientific work finds it an overwhelming reward simply to behold it. In these Laws one stands face to face with truth, solid and unchangeable. Each single Law is an instrument of scientific research, simple in its adjustments, universal in its application, infallible in its results. And despite the limitations of its sphere on every side Law is still the largest, richest, and surest source of human knowledge.

It is not necessary for the present to more than lightly touch on definitions of Natural Law. The Duke of Argyll indicates five senses in which the word is used, but we may content ourselves here by taking it in its most simple and obvious significance. The fundamental conception of Law is an ascertained working sequence or constant order among the Phenomena of Nature. This impression of Law as order it is important to receive in its simplicity, for the idea is often corrupted by having attached to it erroneous views of cause and effect. In its true sense Natural Law predicates nothing of causes. The Laws of Nature are simply statements of the orderly condition of things in Nature, what is found in Nature by a sufficient number of competent observers. What these Laws are in themselves is not agreed. That they have any absolute existence even is far from certain. They are relative to man in his many limitations, and represent for him the constant expression of what he may always expect to find in the world around him. But that they have any causal connection with the things around him is not to be conceived. The Natural Laws originate nothing, sustain nothing; they are merely responsible for uniformity in sustaining what has been originated and what is being sustained. They are modes of operation, therefore, not operators; processes, not powers. The Law of Gravitation, for instance, speaks to science only of process. It has no light to offer as to itself. Newton did not discover Gravity—that is not discovered yet. He discovered its Law, which is Gravitation, but that tells us nothing of its origin, of its nature, or of its cause.

The Natural Laws then are great lines running not only through the world, but, as we now know, through the universe, reducing it like parallels of latitude to intelligent order. In themselves, be it once more repeated, they may have no more absolute existence than parallels of latitude. But they exist for us. They are drawn for us to understand the part by some Hand that drew the whole; so drawn, perhaps, that, understanding the part, we too in time may learn to understand the whole. Now the inquiry we propose to ourselves resolves itself into the simple question, Do these lines stop with what we call the Natural sphere? Is it not possible that they may lead further? Is it probable that the Hand which ruled them gave up the work where most of all they were required? Did that Hand divide the world into two, a cosmos and a chaos, the higher being the chaos? With Nature as the symbol of all of harmony and beauty that is known to man, must we still talk of the super-natural, not as a convenient word, but as a different order of world, an unintelligible world, where the Reign of Mystery supersedes the Reign of Law?

This question, let it be carefully observed, applies to Laws not to Phenomena. That the Phenomena of the Spiritual World are in analogy with the Phenomena of the Natural World requires no restatement. Since Plato enunciated his doctrine of the Cave or of the twice-divided line; since Christ spake in parables; since Plotinus wrote of the world as an imaged image; since the mysticism of Swedenborg; since Bacon and Pascal; since "Sartor Resartus" and "In Memoriam," it has been all but a commonplace with thinkers that "the invisible things of God from the creation of the world are clearly seen, being understood by the things that are made." Milton's question–

> "What if earth
> Be but the shadow of heaven, and things therein
> Each to other like more than on earth is thought?"

–is now superfluous. "In our doctrine of representations and correspondences," says Swedenborg, "we shall treat of both these symbolical and typical resemblances, and of the astonishing things that occur, I will not say in the living body only, but throughout Nature, and which correspond so entirely to supreme and spiritual things, that one would swear that the physical world was purely symbolical of the spiritual world." And Carlyle: "All visible things are emblems. What thou seest is not there on its own account; strictly speaking is not there at all. Matter exists only spiritually, and to represent some idea and body it forth."

But the analogies of Law are a totally different thing from the analogies of Phenomena and have a very different value. To say generally, with Pascal, that "La nature est une image de la grace," is merely to be poetical. The function of Hervey's "Meditations in a Flower Garden," or, Flavel's "Husbandry Spiritualized," is mainly homiletical. That such works have an interest is not to be denied. The place of parable in teaching, and especially after the sanction of the greatest of Teachers, must always be recognised. The very necessities of language indeed demand this method of presenting truth. The temporal is the husk and framework of the eternal, and thoughts can be uttered only through things.

But analogies between Phenomena bear the same relation to analogies of Law that Phenomena themselves bear to Law. The light of Law on truth, as we have seen, is an immense advance upon the light of Phenomena. The discovery of Law is simply the discovery of Science. And if the analogies of Natural Law can be extended to the Spiritual World, that whole region at once falls within the domain of science and secures a basis as well as an illumination in the constitution and course of Nature. All, therefore, that has been claimed for parable can be predicated a fortiori of this—with the addition that a proof on the basis of Law would want no criterion possessed by the most advanced science.

That the validity of analogy generally has been seriously questioned one must frankly own. Doubtless there is much difficulty and even liability to gross error in attempting to establish analogy in specific cases. The value of the likeness appears differently to different minds, and in discussing an individual instance questions of relevancy will invariably crop up. Of course, in the language of John Stuart Mill, "when the analogy can be proved, the argument founded upon it cannot be resisted." But so great is the difficulty of proof that many are compelled to attach the most inferior weight to analogy as a method of reasoning." Analogical evidence is generally more successful in silencing objections than in evincing truth.

Though it rarely refutes it frequently repels refutation; like those weapons which though they cannot kill the enemy, will ward his blows. It must be allowed that analogical evidence is at least but a feeble support, and is hardly ever honoured with the name of proof. Other authorities on the other hand, such as Sir William Hamilton, admit analogy to a primary place in logic and regard it as the very basis of induction.

But, fortunately, we are spared all discussion on this worn subject, for two cogent reasons. For one thing, we do not demand of Nature directly to prove Religion. That was never its function. Its function is to interpret. And this, after all, is possibly the most fruitful proof. The best proof of a thing is that we see it; if we do not see it, perhaps proof will not convince us of it. It is the want of the discerning faculty, the clairvoyant power of seeing the eternal in the temporal, rather than the failure of the reason, that begets the sceptic. But secondly, and more particularly, a significant circumstance has to be taken into account, which, though it will appear more clearly afterwards, may be stated here at once. The position we have been led to take up is not that the Spiritual Laws are analogous to the Natural Laws, but that, they are the same Laws. It is not a question of analogy but of Identity. The Natural Laws are not the shadows or images of the Spiritual in the same sense as autumn is emblematical of Decay, or the falling leaf of Death. The Natural Laws, as the Law of Continuity might well warn us, do not stop with the visible and then give place to a new set of Laws bearing a strong similitude to them.

The Laws of the invisible are the same Laws, projections of the natural not supernatural. Analogous Phenomena are not the fruit of parallel Laws, but of the same Laws—Laws which at one end, as it were, may be dealing with Matter, at the other end with Spirit. As there will be some inconvenience, however, in dispensing with the word analogy, we shall continue occasionally to employ it. Those who apprehend the real relation will mentally substitute the larger term.

Let us now look for a moment at the present state of the question. Can it be said that the Laws of the Spiritual World are in any sense considered even to have analogies with the Natural World? Here and there certainly one finds an attempt, and a successful attempt, to exhibit on a rational basis one or two of the great Moral Principles of the Spiritual World. But the Physical World has not been appealed to. Its magnificent system of Laws remains outside, and its contribution meanwhile is either silently ignored or purposely set aside. The Physical, it is said, is too remote from the Spiritual. The Moral World may afford a basis for religious truth, but even this is often the baldest concession; while the appeal to the Physical universe is everywhere dismissed as, on the face of it, irrelevant and unfruitful. From the scientific side, again, nothing has been done to court a closer fellowship. Science has taken theology at its own estimate. It is a thing apart. The

Spiritual World is not only a different world, but a different kind of world, a world arranged on a totally different principle, under a different governmental scheme.

The Reign of Law has gradually crept into every department of Nature, transforming knowledge everywhere into Science. The process goes on, and Nature slowly appears to us as one great unity, until the borders of the Spiritual World are reached. There the Law of Continuity ceases, and the harmony breaks down. And men who have learned their elementary lessons truly from the alphabet of the lower Laws, going on to seek a higher knowledge, are suddenly confronted with the Great Exception.

Even those who have examined most carefully the relations of the Natural and the Spiritual, seem to have committed themselves deliberately to a final separation in matters of Law. It is a surprise to find such a writer as Horace Bushnell, for instance, describing the Spiritual World as "another system of nature incommunicably separate from ours," and further defining it thus: "God has, in fact, erected another and higher system, that of spiritual being and government for which nature exists; a system not under the law of cause and effect, but ruled and marshalled under other kinds of laws." Few men have shown more insight than Bushnell in illustrating Spiritual truth from the Natural World; but he has not only failed to perceive the analogy with regard to Law, but emphatically denies it.

In the recent literature of this whole region there nowhere seems any advance upon the position of "Nature and the Supernatural." All are agreed in speaking of Nature and the Supernatural. Nature in the Supernatural, so far as Laws are concerned, is still an unknown truth.

"The Scientific Basis of Faith" is a suggestive title. The accomplished author announces that the object of his investigation is to show that "the world of nature and mind, as made known by science, constitute a basis and a preparation for that highest moral and spiritual life of man, which is evoked by the self-revelation of God." On the whole, Mr. Murphy seems to be more philosophical and more profound in his view of the relation of science and religion than any writer of modern times. His conception of religion is broad and lofty, his acquaintance with science adequate. He makes constant, admirable, and often original use of analogy; and yet, in spite of the promise of this quotation, he has failed to find any analogy in that department of Law where surely, of all others, it might most reasonably be looked for. In the broad subject even of the analogies of what he defines as "evangelical religion" with Nature, Mr. Murphy discovers nothing. Nor can this be traced either to short-sight or over-sight. The subject occurs to him more than once, and he deliberately dismisses it—dismisses it not merely as unfruitful, but with a distinct denial of its relevancy. The memorable paragraph from Origin which forms the text of Butler's "Analogy," he calls "this shallow and false saying." He says: "The designation of Butler's scheme of religious philosophy ought then to be the analogy of religion, legal and evangelical, to the constitution of nature. But does this give altogether a true meaning? Does this double analogy really exist?

"If justice is natural law among beings having a moral nature, there is the closest analogy between the constitution of nature and merely legal religion. Legal religion is only the extension of natural justice into a future life. . . . But is this true of evangelical religion? Have the doctrines of Divine grace any similar support in the analogies of nature? I trow not."

And with reference to a specific question, speaking of immortality, he asserts that "the analogies of mere nature are opposed to the doctrine of immortality."

With regard to Butler's great work in this department, it is needless at this time of day to point out that his aims did not lie exactly in this direction. He did not seek to indicate analogies between religion and the constitution and course of Nature. His theme was, "The Analogy of Religion to the constitution and course of Nature." And although he pointed out direct analogies of Phenomena, such as those between the metamorphoses of insects and the doctrine of a future state; and although he showed that "the natural and moral constitution and government of the world are so connected as to make up together but one scheme," his real intention was not so much to construct arguments as to repel objections. His emphasis accordingly was laid upon the difficulties of the two schemes rather than on their positive lines; and so thoroughly has he made out his point, that as is well known, the effect upon many has been, not to lead them to accept the Spiritual World on the ground of the Natural, but to make them despair of both. Butler lived at a time when defence was more necessary than construction, when the materials for construction were scarce and insecure, and when, besides. Some of the things to be defended were quite incapable of defence. Notwithstanding this, his influence over the whole field since has been unparalleled.

After all, then, the Spiritual World, as it appears at this moment, is outside Natural Law. Theology continues to be considered, as it has always been, a thing apart. It remains still a stupendous and splendid construction, but on lines altogether its own. Nor is Theology to be blamed for this. Nature has been long in speaking; even yet its voice is low, sometimes inaudible. Science is the true defaulter, for Theology had to wait patiently for its development. As the highest of the sciences, Theology in the order of evolution should be the last to fall into rank. It is reserved for it to perfect the final harmony. Still, if it continues longer to remain a thing apart, with increasing reason will be such protests as this of the "Unseen Universe," when, in speaking of a view of miracles held by an older Theology, it declares:—"If he submits to be guided by such interpreters, each intelligent being will for ever continue to be baffled in any attempt to explain these phenomena, because they are said to have no physical relation to anything that went before or that followed after; in fine, they are made to form a universe within a universe, a portion cut off by an insurmountable barrier from the domain of scientific inquiry."

This is the secret of the present decadence of Religion in the world of Science. For Science can hear nothing of a Great Exception. Constructions on unique lines, "portions cut off by an insurmountable barrier from the domain of scientific inquiry," it dare not recognise. Nature has taught it this lesson, and Nature is right. It is the province of Science to vindicate Nature here at any hazard. But in blaming Theology for its intolerance, it has been betrayed into an intolerance less excusable. It has pronounced upon it too soon. What if Religion be yet brought within the sphere of Law? Law is the revelation of time. One by one slowly through the centuries the Sciences have crystallized into geometrical form, each form not only perfect in itself, but perfect in its relation to all other forms. Many forms had to be perfected before the form of the Spiritual. The Inorganic has to be worked out before the Organic, the Natural before the Spiritual. Theology at present has merely an ancient and provisional philosophic form. By and by it will be seen whether it be not susceptible of another. For Theology must pass through the necessary stages of progress, like any other science. The method of science-making is now fully established. In almost all cases the natural history and development are the same. Take, for example, the case of Geology. A century ago there was none. Science went out to look for it, and brought back a Geology which, if Nature were a harmony, had falsehood written almost on its face. It was the Geology of Catastrophism, a Geology so out of line with Nature as revealed by the other sciences, that on a priori grounds a thoughtful mind might have been justified in dismissing it as a final form of any science. And its fallacy was soon and thoroughly exposed. The advent of modified uniformitarian principles all but banished the word catastrophe from science, and marked the birth of Geology as we know it now. Geology, that is to say, had fallen at last into the great scheme of Law. Religious doctrines, many of them at least, have been up to this time all but as catastrophic as the old Geology. They are not on the lines of Nature as we have learned to decipher her. If any one feel, as Science complains that it feels, that the lie of things in the Spiritual World as arranged by Theology is not in harmony with the world around, is not, in short, scientific, he is entitled to raise the question whether this be really the final form of those departments of Theology to which his complaint refers, He is justified, moreover, in demanding a new investigation with all modern methods and resources; and Science is bound by its principles not less than by the lessons of its own past, to suspend judgment till the last attempt is made. The success of such an attempt will be looked forward to with hopefulness or fearfulness just in proportion to one's confidence in Nature—in proportion to one's belief in the divinity of man and in the divinity of things. If there is any truth in the unity of Nature, in that supreme principle of Continuity which is growing in splendour with every discovery of science, the conclusion is foregone. If there is any foundation for Theology, if the phenomena of the Spiritual World are real, in the nature of things they ought to come into the sphere of Law. Such is at once the demand of Science upon Religion and the prophecy that it can and shall be fulfilled.

The Botany of Linnaeus, a purely artificial system, was a splendid contribution to human knowledge, and did more in its day to enlarge the view of the vegetable kingdom than all that had gone before. But all artificial systems must pass away. None knew better than the great Swedish naturalist himself that his system, being artificial, was but provisional. Nature must be read in its own light. And as the botanical field became more luminous, the system of Jussieu and De Candolle slowly emerged as a native growth, unfolded itself as naturally as the petals of one of its own flowers, and forcing itself upon men's intelligence as the very voice of Nature, banished the Linnaean system for ever. It were unjust to say that the present Theology is as artificial as the system of Linnaeus; in many particulars it wants but a fresh expression to make it in the most modern sense scientific. But if it has a basis in the constitution and course of Nature, that basis has never been adequately shown. It has depended on Authority rather than on Law; and a new basis must be sought and found if it is to be presented to those with whom Law alone is Authority.

It is not of course to be inferred that the scientific method will ever abolish the radical distinctions of the Spiritual World. True science proposes to itself no such general levelling in any department. Within the unity of the whole there must always be room for the characteristic differences of the parts, and those tendencies of thought at the present time which ignore such distinctions, in their zeal for simplicity really create confusion. As has been well-said by Mr. Hutton: "Any attempt to merge the distinctive characteristic of a higher science in a lower—of chemical changes in mechanical—of physiological in chemical—above all, of mental changes in physiological—is a neglect of the radical assumption of all science, because it is an attempt to deduce representations—or rather misrepresentations—of one kind of phenomenon from a conception of another kind which does not contain it, and must have it implicitly and illicitly smuggled in before it can be extracted out of it. Hence, instead of increasing our means of representing the universe to ourselves without the detailed examination of particulars, such a procedure leads to misconstructions of fact on the basis of an imported theory, and generally ends in forcibly perverting the least known science to the type of the better known."

What is wanted is simply a unity of conception, but not such a unity of conception as should be founded on an absolute identity of phenomena. This latter might indeed be a unity, but it would be a very tame one The perfection of unity is attained where there is infinite variety of phenomena, infinite complexity of relation, but great simplicity of Law. Science will be complete when all known phenomena can be arranged in one vast circle in which a few well known Laws shall form the radii—these radii at once separating and uniting, separating into particular groups, yet uniting all to a common centre. To show that the radii for some of the most characteristic phenomena of the Spiritual World are already drawn within that circle by science is the main object of the papers which follow. There will be found an attempt to re-state a few of the more elementary facts of the Spiritual Life in terms of Biology. Any argument for Natural Law in the Spiritual World may be best tested in the "a posteriori" form. And although the succeeding pages are not designed in the first instance to prove a principle, they may yet be entered here as evidence. The practical test is a severe one, but on that account all the more satisfactory.

And what will be gained if the point be made out? Not a few things. For one, as partly indicated already, the scientific demand of the age will be satisfied. That demand is that all that concerns life and conduct shall be placed on a scientific basis. The only great attempt to meet that at present is Positivism.

But what again is a scientific basis? What exactly is this demand of the age? "By Science I understand," says Huxley, "all knowledge which rests upon evidence and reasoning of a like character to that which claims our assent to ordinary scientific propositions; and if any one is able to make good the assertion that his theology rests upon valid evidence and sound reasoning, then it appears to me that such theology must take its place as a part of science." That the assertion has been already made good is claimed by many who deserve to be heard on questions of scientific evidence. But if more is wanted by some minds, more not perhaps of a higher kind but of a different kind, at least the attempt can be made to gratify them. Mr. Frederic Harrison, in name of the Positive method of thought, "turns aside from ideal standards which avow themselves to be lawless, which profess to transcend the field of law. We say life and conduct shall stand for us wholly on a basis of law, and must rest entirely in that region of science (not physical, but moral and social science) where we are free to use our intelligence, in the methods known to us as intelligible logic, methods which the intellect can analyse. When you confront us with hypotheses, however sublime and however affecting, if they cannot be stated in terms of the rest of our knowledge, if they are disparate to that world of sequence and sensation which to us is the ultimate base of all our real knowledge, then we shake our heads and turn aside." This is a most reasonable demand, and we humbly accept the challenge. We think religious truth, or at all events certain of the largest facts of the Spiritual Life, can be stated "in terms of the rest of our knowledge."

We do not say, as already hinted, that the proposal includes an attempt to prove the existence of the Spiritual World. Does that need proof? And if so, what sort of evidence would be considered in court? The facts of the Spiritual World are as real to thousands as the facts of the Natural World–and more real to hundreds. But were one asked to prove that the Spiritual World can be discerned by the appropriate faculties, one would do it precisely as one would attempt to prove the Natural World to be an object of recognition to the senses–and with as much or as little success. In either instance probably the fact would be found incapable of demonstration, but not more in the one case than in the other. Were one asked to prove the existence of Spiritual Life, one would also do it exactly as one would seek to prove Natural Life. And this perhaps might be attempted with more hope.

But this is not on the immediate programme. Science deals with known facts; and accepting certain known facts in the Spiritual World we proceed to arrange them, to discover their Laws, to inquire if they can be stated "in terms of the rest of our knowledge."

At the same time, although attempting no philosophical proof of the existence of a Spiritual Life and a Spiritual World, we are not without hope that the general line of thought here may be useful to some who are honestly inquiring in these directions. The stumbling-block to most minds is perhaps less the mere existence of the unseen than the want of definition, the apparently hopeless vagueness, and not least, the delight in this vagueness as mere vagueness by some who look upon this as the mark of quality in Spiritual things. It will be at least something to tell earnest seekers that the Spiritual World is not a castle in the air, of an architecture unknown to earth or heaven, but a fair ordered realm furnished with many familiar things and ruled by well-remembered Laws.

It is scarcely necessary to emphasise under a second head the gain in clearness. The Spiritual World as it stands is full of perplexity. One can escape doubt only by escaping thought. With regard to many important articles of religion perhaps the best and the worst course at present open to a doubter is simple credulity. Who is to answer for this state of things?

It comes as a necessary tax for improvement on the age in which we live. The old ground of faith, Authority, is given up; the new, Science, has not yet taken its place. Men did not require to see truth before; they only needed to believe it. Truth, therefore, had not been put by Theology in a seeing form—which, however, was its original form. But now they ask to see it. And when it is shown them they start back in despair. We shall not say what they see. But we shall say what they might see. If the Natural Laws were run through the Spiritual World, they might see the great lines of religious truth as clearly and simply as the broad lines of science. As they gazed into that Natural-Spiritual World they would say to themselves, "We have seen something like this before. This order is known to us. It is not arbitrary. This Law here is that old Law there, and this Phenomenon here, what can it be but that which stood in precisely the same relation to that Law yonder?" And so gradually from the new form everything assumes new meaning. So the Spiritual World becomes slowly Natural; and, what is of all but equal moment, the Natural World becomes slowly Spiritual. Nature is not a mere image or emblem of the Spiritual. It is a working model of the Spiritual. In the Spiritual World the same wheels revolve—but without the iron. The same figures flit across the stage, the same processes of growth go on, the same functions are discharged, the same biological laws prevail—only with a different quality of Bios. Plato's prisoner, if not out of the Cave, has at least his face to the light.

> "The earth is cram'd with heaven,
> And every common bush afire with God."

How much of the Spiritual World is covered by Natural law we do not propose at present to inquire. It is certain, at least, that the whole is not covered. And nothing more lends confidence to the method than this. For one thing, room is still left for mystery. Had no place remained for mystery it had proved itself both unscientific and irreligious. A Science without mystery is unknown; a Religion without mystery is absurd. This is no attempt to reduce Religion to a question of mathematics, or demonstrate God in biological formulae. The elimination of mystery from the universe is the elimination of Religion. However far the scientific method may penetrate the Spiritual World, there will always remain a region to be explored by a scientific faith. "I shall never rise to the point of view which wishes to 'raise' faith to knowledge. To me, the way of truth is to come through the knowledge of my ignorance to the submissiveness of faith, and then, making that my starting place, to raise my knowledge into faith."

Lest this proclamation of mystery should seem alarming, let us add that this mystery also is scientific. The one subject on which all scientific men are agreed the one theme on which all alike become eloquent, the one strain of pathos in all their writing and speaking and thinking, concerns that final uncertainty, that utter blackness of darkness bounding their work on every side. If the light of Nature is to illuminate for us the Spiritual Sphere, there may well be a black Unknown, corresponding, at least at some points, to this zone of darkness round the Natural World.

But the final gain would appear in the department of Theology. The establishment of the Spiritual Laws on "the solid ground of Nature," to which the mind trusts "which builds for aye," would offer a new basis for certainty in Religion. It has been indicated that the authority of Authority is waning. This is a plain fact. And it was inevitable. Authority—man's Authority, that is—is for children. And there necessarily comes a time when they add to the question, What shall I do? or, What shall I believe? the adult's interrogation—Why? Now this question is sacred, and must be answered.

"How truly its central position is impregnable," Herbert Spencer has well discerned, "religion has never adequately realized. In the devoutest faith, as we habitually see it, there lies hidden an innermost core of scepticism; and it is this scepticism which causes that dread of inquiry displayed by religion when face to face with science." True indeed; Religion has never realized how impregnable are many of its positions. It has not yet been placed on that basis which would make them impregnable. And in a transition period like the present, holding Authority with one hand, the other feeling all around in the darkness for some strong new support, Theology is surely to be pitied. Whence this dread when brought face to face with Science? It cannot be dread of scientific fact. No single fact in Science has ever discredited a fact in Religion. The theologian knows that, and admits that he has no fear of facts. What then has Science done to make Theology tremble? It is its method. It is its system. It is its Reign of Law. It is its harmony and continuity. The attack is not specific. No one point is assailed. It is the whole system which when compared with the other and weighed in its balance is found wanting. An eye which has looked at the first cannot look upon this. To do that, and rest in the contemplation, it has just to uncentury itself.

Herbert Spencer points out further, with how much truth need not now be discussed, that the purification of Religion has always come from Science. It is very apparent at all events that an immense debt must soon be contracted The shifting of the furnishings will be a work of time. But it must be accomplished. And not the least result of the process will be the effect upon Science itself. No department of knowledge ever contributes to another without receiving its own again with usury—witness the reciprocal favours of Biology and Sociology. From the time that Comte defined the analogy between the phenomena exhibited by aggregations of associated men and those of animal colonies, the Science of Life and the Science of Society have been so contributing to one another that their progress since has been all but hand-in-hand. A conception borrowed by the one has been observed in time finding its way back, and always in an enlarged form, to further illuminate and enrich the field it left. So must it be with Science and Religion. If the purification of Religion comes from Science, the purification of Science, in a deeper sense, shall come from Religion. The true ministry of Nature must at last be honoured, and Science take its place as the great expositor. To Men of Science, not less than to Theologians,

"Science then
Shall be a precious visitant; and then,
And only then, be worthy of her name:
For then her heart shall kindle, her dull eye,
Dull and inanimate, no more shall hang
Chained to its object in brute slavery;
But taught with patient interest to watch
The process of things, and serve the cause
Of order and distinctness, not for this
Shall it forget that its most noble use,
Its most illustrious province, must be found
In furnishing clear guidance, a support,
Not treacherous, to the mind's excursive power."

But the gift of Science to Theology shall be not less rich. With the inspiration of Nature to illuminate what the inspiration of Revelation has left obscure, heresy in certain whole departments shall become impossible. With the demonstration of the naturalness of the supernatural, scepticism even may come to be regarded as unscientific. And those who have wrestled long for a few bare truths to ennoble life and rest their souls in thinking of the future will not be left in doubt.

It is impossible to believe that the amazing succession of revelations in the domain of Nature during the last few centuries, at which the world has all but grown tired wondering, are to yield nothing for the higher life. If the development of doctrine is to have any meaning for the future, Theology must draw upon the further revelation of the seen for the further revelation of the unseen. It need, and can, add nothing to fact; but as the vision of Newton rested on a clearer and richer world than that of Plato, so, though seeing the same things in the Spiritual World as our fathers, we may see them clearer and richer. With the work of the centuries upon it, the mental eye is a finer instrument, and demands a more ordered world. Had the revelation of Law been given sooner, it had been unintelligible. Revelation never volunteers anything that man could discover for himself—on the principle, probably, that it is only when he is capable of discovering it that he is capable of appreciating it. Besides, children do not need Laws, except Laws in the sense of commandments. They repose with simplicity on authority, and ask no questions. But there comes a time, as the world reaches its manhood, when they will ask questions, and stake, moreover, everything on the answers. That time is now. Hence we must exhibit our doctrines, not lying athwart the lines of the world's thinking, in a place reserved, and therefore shunned, for the Great Exception; but in their kinship to all truth and in their Law-relation to the whole of Nature. This is, indeed, simply following out the system of teaching begun by Christ Himself. And what is the search for spiritual truth in the Laws of Nature but an attempt to utter the parables which have been hid so long in the world around without a preacher, and to tell men once more that the Kingdom of Heaven is like unto this and to that?

Part II

The Law of Continuity having been referred to already as a prominent factor in this inquiry, it may not be out of place to sustain the plea for Natural Law in the Spiritual Sphere by a brief statement and application of this great principle. The Law of Continuity furnishes an a priori argument for the position we are attempting to establish of the most convincing kind—of such a kind, indeed, as to seem to our mind final. Briefly indicated, the ground taken up is this, that if Nature be a harmony, Man in all his relations–physical, mental, moral, and spiritual–falls to be included within its circle. It is altogether unlikely that man spiritual should be violently separated in all the conditions of growth, development, and life, from man physical. It is indeed difficult to conceive that one set of principles should guide the natural life, and these at a certain period– the very point where they are needed–suddenly give place to another set of principles altogether new and unrelated. Nature has never taught us to expect such a catastrophe. She has nowhere prepared us for it. And Man cannot in the nature of things, in the nature of thought, in the nature of language, be separated into two such incoherent halves.

The spiritual man, it is true, is to be studied in a different department of science from the natural man. But the harmony established by science is not a harmony within specific departments. It is the universe that is the harmony, the universe of which these are but parts. And the harmonies of the parts depend for all their weight and interest on the harmony of the whole. While, therefore, there are many harmonies, there is but one harmony. The breaking up of the phenomena of the universe into carefully guarded groups, and the allocation of certain prominent Laws to each, it must never be forgotten, and however much Nature lends herself to it, are artificial. We find an evolution in Botany, another in Geology, and another in Astronomy, and the effect is to lead one insensibly to look upon these as three distinct evolutions. But these sciences, of course, are mere departments created by ourselves to facilitate knowledge–reductions of Nature to the scale of our own intelligence. And we must beware of breaking up Nature except for this purpose. Science has so dissected everything, that it becomes a mental difficulty to put the puzzle together again; and we must keep ourselves in practice by constantly thinking of Nature as a whole, if science is not to be spoiled by its own refinements. Evolution being found in so many different sciences, the likelihood is that it is a universal principle.

And there is no presumption whatever against this Law and many others being excluded from the domain of the spiritual life. On the other hand, there are very convincing reasons why the Natural Laws should be continuous through the Spiritual Sphere—not changed in any way to meet the new circumstances, but continuous as they stand.

But to the exposition. One of the most striking generalisations of recent science is that even Laws have their Law. Phenomena first, in the progress of knowledge, were grouped together, and Nature shortly presented the spectacle of a cosmos, the lines of beauty being the great Natural Laws. So long, however, as these Laws were merely great lines running through Nature, so long as they remained isolated from one another, the system of Nature was still incomplete. The principle which sought Law among phenomena had to go further and seek a Law among the Laws. Laws themselves accordingly came to be treated as they treated phenomena, and found themselves finally grouped in a still narrower circle. That inmost circle is governed by one great Law, the Law of Continuity. It is the Law for Laws.

It is perhaps significant that few exact definitions of Continuity are to be found. Even in Sir W. R. Grove's famous paper, the fountainhead of the modern form of this far from modern truth, there is no attempt at definition. In point of fact, its sweep is so magnificent, it appeals so much more to the imagination than to the reason, that men have preferred to exhibit rather than to define it. Its true greatness consists in the final impression it leaves on the mind with regard to the uniformity of Nature. For it was reserved for the Law of Continuity to put the finishing touch to the harmony of the universe.

Probably the most satisfactory way to secure for oneself a just appreciation of the Principle of Continuity is to try to conceive the universe without it. The opposite of a continuous universe would be a discontinuous universe, an incoherent and irrelevant universe—as irrelevant in all its ways of doing things as an irrelevant person. In effect, to withdraw Continuity from the universe would be the same as to withdraw reason from an individual. The universe would run deranged; the world would be a mad world.

There used to be a children's book which bore the fascinating title of "The Chance World." It described a world in which everything happened by chance. The sun might rise or it might not; or it might appear at any hour, or the moon might come up instead. When children were born they might have one head or a dozen heads, and those heads might not be on their shoulders—there might be no shoulders—but arranged about the limbs. If one jumped up in the air it was impossible to predict whether he would ever come down again. That he came down yesterday was no guarantee that he would do it next time. For every day antecedent and consequent varied, and gravitation and everything else changed from hour to hour. Today a child's body might be so light that it was impossible for it to descend from its chair to the floor; but tomorrow, in attempting the experiment again, the impetus might drive it through a three-storey house and dash it to pieces somewhere near the centre of the earth. In this chance world cause and effect were abolished. Law was annihilated. And the result to the inhabitants of such a world could only be that reason would be impossible. It would be a lunatic world with a population of lunatics.

Now this is no more than a real picture of what the world would be without Law, or the universe without Continuity. And hence we come in sight of the necessity of some principle or Law according to which Laws shall be, and be "continuous" throughout the system. Man as a rational and moral being demands a pledge that if he depends on Nature for any given result on the ground that Nature has previously led him to expect such a result, his intellect shall not be insulted, nor his confidence in her abused. If he is to trust Nature, in short, it must be guaranteed to him that in doing so he will "never be put to confusion." The authors of the Unseen Universe conclude their examination of this principle by saying that "assuming the existence of a supreme Governor of the universe, the Principle of Continuity may be said to be the definite expression in words of our trust that He will not put us to permanent intellectual confusion, and we can easily conceive similar expressions of trust with reference to the other faculties of man." Or, as it has been well put elsewhere, Continuity is the expression of "the Divine Veracity in Nature." The most striking examples of the continuousness of Law are perhaps those furnished by Astronomy, especially in connection with the more recent applications of spectrum analysis. But even in the case of the simpler Laws the demonstration is complete. There is no reason apart from Continuity to expect that gravitation for instance should prevail outside our world. But wherever matter has been detected throughout the entire universe, whether in the form of star or planet, comet or meteorite, it is found to obey that Law. "If there were no other indication of unity than this, it would be almost enough. For the unity which is implied in the mechanism of the heavens is indeed a unity which is all-embracing and complete. The structure of our own bodies, with all that depends upon it, is a structure governed by, and therefore adapted to, the same force of gravitation which has determined the form and the movements of myriads of worlds. Every part of the human organism is fitted to conditions which would all be destroyed in a moment if the forces of gravitation were to change or fail."

But it is unnecessary to multiply illustrations. Having defined the principle we may proceed at once to apply it. And the argument may be summed up in a sentence. As the Natural Laws are continuous through the universe of matter and of space, so will they be continuous through the universe of spirit.

If this be denied, what then? Those who deny it must furnish the disproof. The argument is founded on a principle which is now acknowledged to be universal; and the onus of disproof must lie with those who may be bold enough to take up the position that a region exists where at last the Principle of Continuity fails. To do this one would first have to overturn Nature, then science, and last, the human mind.

It may seem an obvious objection that many of the Natural

Laws have no connection whatever with the Spiritual World, and as a matter of fact are not continued through it. Gravitation for instance–what direct application has that in the Spiritual World? The reply is threefold. First, there is no proof that it does not hold there. If the spirit be in any sense material it certainly must hold. In the second place, gravitation may hold for the Spiritual Sphere although it cannot be directly proved. The spirit may be armed with powers which enable it to rise superior to gravity. During the action of these powers gravity need be no more suspended than in the case of a plant which rises in the air during the process of growth. It does this in virtue of a higher Law and in apparent defiance of the lower. Thirdly, if the spiritual be not material it still cannot be said that gravitation ceases at that point to be continuous. It is not gravitation that ceases–it is matter.

This point, however, will require development for another reason. In the case of the plant just referred to, there is a principle of growth or vitality at work superseding the attraction of gravity. Why is there no trace of that Law in the Inorganic world? Is not this another instance of the discontinuousness of Law? If the Law of vitality has so little connection with the Inorganic kingdom–less even than gravitation with the Spiritual, what becomes of Continuity? Is it not evident that each kingdom of Nature has its own set of Laws which continue possibly untouched for the specific kingdom but never extend beyond it?

It is quite true that when we pass from the Inorganic to the Organic, we come upon a new set of Laws. But the reason why the lower set do not seem to act in the higher sphere is not that they are annihilated, but that they are overruled. And the reason why the higher Laws are not found operating in the lower is not because they are not continuous downwards, but because there is nothing for them there to act upon. It is not Law that fails, but opportunity. The biological Laws are continuous for life. Wherever there is life, that is to say, they will be found acting, just as gravitation acts wherever there is matter.

We have purposely, in the last paragraph, indulged in a fallacy. We have said that the biological Laws would certainly be continuous in the lower or mineral sphere were there anything there for them to act upon. Now Laws do not act upon anything. It has been stated already, although apparently it cannot be too abundantly emphasized, that Laws are only codes of operation, not themselves operators. The accurate statement, therefore, would be that the biological Laws would be continuous in the lower sphere were there anything there for them, not to act upon, but to keep in order. If there is no acting going on, if there is nothing being kept in order, the responsibility does not lie with Continuity. The Law will always be at its post, not only when its services are required, but wherever they are possible.

Attention is drawn to this, for it is a correction one will find oneself compelled often to make in his thinking. It is so difficult to keep out of mind the idea of substance in connection with the Natural Laws, the idea that they are the movers, the essences, the energies, that one is constantly on the verge of falling into false conclusions. Thus a hasty glance at the present argument on the part of any one ill-furnished enough to confound Law with substance or with cause would probably lead to its immediate rejection.

For, to continue the same line of illustration, it might next be urged that such a Law as Biogenesis, which, as we hope to show afterwards, is the fundamental Law of life for both the natural and spiritual worlds, can have no application whatsoever in the latter sphere. The life with which it deals in the Natural World does not enter at all into the Spiritual World, and therefore, it might be argued, the Law of Biogenesis cannot be capable of extension into it. The Law of Continuity seems to be snapped at the point where the natural passes into the spiritual. The vital principle of the body is a different thing from the vital principle of the spiritual life. Biogenesis deals with Bios, with the natural life, with cells and germs, and as there are no exactly similar cells and germs in the Spiritual World, the Law cannot therefore apply. All which is as true as if one were to say that the fifth proposition of the First

Book of Euclid applies when the figures are drawn with chalk upon a blackboard, but fails with regard to structures of wood or stone.

The proposition is continuous for the whole world, and, doubtless, likewise for the sun and moon and stars. The same universality may be predicated likewise for the Law of life. Wherever there is life we may expect to find it arranged, ordered, governed according to the same Law. At the beginning of the natural life we find the Law that natural life can only come from pre-existing natural life; and at the beginning of the spiritual life we find that the spiritual life can only come from pre-existing spiritual life. But there are not two Laws; there is one—Biogenesis. At one end the Law is dealing with matter, at the other with spirit. The qualitative terms natural and spiritual make no difference. Biogenesis is the Law for all life and for all kinds of life, and the particular substance with which it is associated is as indifferent to Biogenesis as it is to Gravitation. Gravitation will act whether the substance be suns and stars, or grains of sand, or raindrops. Biogenesis, in like manner, will act wherever there is life.

The conclusion finally is, that from the nature of Law in general, and from the scope of the Principle of Continuity in particular, the Laws of the natural life must be those of the spiritual life. This does not exclude, observe, the possibility of there being new Laws in addition within the Spiritual Sphere; nor does it even include the supposition that the old Laws will be the conspicuous Laws of the Spiritual World, both which points will be dealt with presently. It simply asserts that whatever else may be found, these must be found there; that they must be there though they may not be seen there, and that they must project beyond there if there be anything beyond there. If the Law of Continuity is true, the only way to escape the conclusion that the Laws of the natural life are the Laws, or at least are Laws, of the spiritual life, is to say that there is no spiritual life. It is really easier to give up the phenomena than to give up the Law.

Two questions now remain for further consideration—one

bearing on the possibility of new Law in the spiritual; the other, on the assumed invisibility or inconspicuousness of the old Laws on account of their subordination to the new.

Let us begin by conceding that there may be new Laws. The argument might then be advanced that since, in Nature generally, we come upon new Laws as we pass from lower to higher kingdoms, the old still remaining in force, the newer Laws which one would expect to meet in the Spiritual World would so transcend and overwhelm the older as to make the analogy or identity, even if traced, of no practical use. The new Laws would represent operations and energies so different, and so much more elevated, that they would afford the true keys to the Spiritual World. As Gravitation is practically lost sight of when we pass into the domain of life, so Biogenesis would be lost sight of as we enter the Spiritual Sphere.

We must first separate in this statement the old confusion of Law and energy. Gravitation is not lost sight of in the organic world. Gravity may be, to a certain extent, but not Gravitation; and gravity only where a higher power counteracts its action. At the same time it is not to be denied that the conspicuous thing in Organic Nature is not the great Inorganic Law.

But the objection turns upon the statement that reasoning from analogy we should expect, in turn, to lose sight of Biogenesis as we enter the Spiritual Sphere. One answer to which is that, as a matter of fact, we do not lose sight of it. So far from being invisible, it lies across the very threshold of the Spiritual World, and, as we shall see, pervades it everywhere. What we lose sight of, to a certain extent, is the natural Bios. In the Spiritual World that is not the conspicuous thing, and it is obscure there just as gravity becomes obscure in the Organic, because something higher, more potent, more characteristic of the higher plane, comes in. That there are higher energies, so to speak, in the Spiritual World is, of course, to be affirmed alike on the ground of analogy and of experience; but it does not follow that these necessitate other Laws. A Law has nothing to do with potency. We may lose sight of a substance, or of an energy, but it is an abuse of language to talk of losing sight of Laws.

Are there, then, no other Laws in the Spiritual World except those which are the projections or extensions of Natural Laws? From the number of Natural Laws which are found in the higher sphere, from the large territory actually embraced by them, and from their special prominence throughout the whole region, it may at least be answered that the margin left for them is small. But if the objection is pressed that it is contrary to the analogy, and unreasonable in itself, that there should not be new Laws for this higher sphere, the reply is obvious. Let these Laws be produced. If the spiritual nature, in inception, growth, and development, does not follow natural principles, let the true principles be stated and explained. We have not denied that there may be new Laws. One would almost be surprised if there were not. The mass of material handed over from the natural to the spiritual, continuous, apparently, from the natural to the spiritual, is so great that till that is worked out it will be impossible to say what space is still left unembraced by Laws that are known. At present it is impossible even approximately to estimate the size of that supposed "terra incognita." From one point of view it ought to be vast, from another extremely small. But however large the region governed by the suspected new Laws may be that cannot diminish by a hair's breadth the size of the territory where the old Laws still prevail. That territory itself, relatively to us though perhaps not absolutely, must be of great extent. The size of the key which is to open it, that is, the size of all the Natural Laws which can be found to apply, is a guarantee that the region of the knowable in the Spiritual World is at least as wide as these regions of the Natural World which by the help of these Laws have been explored. No doubt also there yet remain some Natural Laws to be discovered, and these in time may have a further light to shed on the spiritual field. Then we may know all that is? By no means. We may only know all that may be known. And that may be very little. The Sovereign Will which sways the sceptre of that invisible empire must be granted a right of freedom—that freedom which by putting it into our wills He surely teaches us to honour in His. In much of His dealing with us also, in what may be called the paternal relation, there may seem no special Law—no Law except the highest of all, that Law of which all other Laws are parts, that Law which neither Nature can wholly reflect nor the mind begin to fathom—the Law of Love. He adds nothing to that, however, who loses sight of all other Laws in that, nor does he take from it who finds specific Laws everywhere radiating from it.

With regard to the supposed new Laws of the Spiritual World—those Laws, that is, which are found for the first time in the Spiritual World, and have no analogies lower down—there is this to be said, that there is one strong reason against exaggerating either their number or importance—their importance at least for our immediate needs. The connection between language and the Law of Continuity has been referred to incidentally already. It is clear that we can only express the Spiritual Laws in language borrowed from the visible universe. Being dependent for our vocabulary on images, if an altogether new and foreign set of Laws existed in the Spiritual World, they could never take shape as definite ideas from mere want of words. The hypothetical new Laws which may remain to be discovered in the domain of Natural or Mental Science may afford some index of these hypothetical higher Laws, but this would of course mean that the latter were no longer foreign but in analogy, or, likelier still, identical.

If, on the other hand, the Natural Laws of the future have nothing to say of these higher Laws, what can be said of them? Where is the language to come from in which to frame them? If their disclosure could be of any practical use to us, we may be sure the clue to them, the revelation of them, in some way would have been put into Nature. If, on the contrary, they are not to be of immediate use to man, it is better they should not embarrass him. After all, then, our knowledge of higher Law must be limited by our knowledge of the lower. The Natural Laws as at present known, whatever additions may yet be made to them, give a fair rendering of the facts of Nature. And their analogies or their projections in the Spiritual sphere may also be said to offer a fair account of that sphere, or of one or two conspicuous departments of it. The time has come for that account to be given. The greatest among the theological Laws are the Laws of Nature in disguise. It will be the splendid task of the theology of the future to take off the mask and disclose to a waning scepticism the naturalness of the supernatural.

It is almost singular that the identification of the Laws of the Spiritual World with the Laws of Nature should so long have escaped recognition. For apart from the probability on a priori grounds, it is involved in the whole structure of Parable. When any two Phenomena in the two spheres are seen to be analogous, the parallelism must depend upon the fact that the Laws governing them are not analogous but identical. And yet this basis for Parable seems to have been overlooked. Thus Principal Shairp:

> "This seeing of Spiritual truths mirrored in the face of Nature rests not on any fancied, but in a real analogy between the natural and the spiritual worlds. They are in some sense which science has not ascertained, but which the vital and religious imagination can perceive, counterparts one of the other."

But is not this the explanation, that parallel Phenomena depend upon identical Laws? It is a question indeed whether one can speak of Laws at all as being analogous. Phenomena are parallel, Laws which make them so are themselves one.

In discussing the relations of the Natural and Spiritual kingdom, it has been all but implied hitherto that the Spiritual Laws were framed originally on the plan of the Natural; and the impression one might receive in studying the two worlds for the first time from the side of analogy would naturally be that the lower world was formed first, as a kind of scaffolding on which the higher and Spiritual should be afterwards raised. Now the exact opposite has been the case. The first in the field was the Spiritual World.

It is not necessary to reproduce here in detail the argument which has been stated recently with so much force in the "Unseen Universe." The conclusion of that wort remains still unassailed, that the visible universe has been developed from the unseen. Apart from the general proof from the Law of Continuity, the more special grounds of such a conclusion are, first, the fact insisted upon by Herschel and Clerk-Maxwell that the atoms of which the visible universe is built up bear distinct marks of being manufactured articles; and, secondly, the origin in time of the visible universe is implied from known facts with regard to the dissipation of energy. With the gradual aggregation of mass the energy of the universe has been slowly disappearing, and this loss of energy must go on until none remains. There is, therefore, a point in time when the energy of the universe must come to an end; and that which has its end in time cannot be infinite, it must also have had a beginning in time. Hence the unseen existed before the seen.

There is nothing so especially exalted therefore in the Natural Laws in themselves as to make one anxious to find them blood relations of the Spiritual. It is not only because these Laws are on the ground, more accessible therefore to us who are but groundlings; not only, as the "Unseen Universe" points out in another connection, "because they are at the bottom of the list—are in fact the simplest and lowest—that they are capable of being most readily grasped by the finite intelligences of the universe." But their true significance lies in the fact that they are on the list at all, and especially in that the list is the same list. Their dignity is not as Natural Laws, but as Spiritual Laws, Laws which, as already said, at one end are dealing with Matter, and at the other with Spirit. "The physical properties of matter form the alphabet which is put into our hands by God, the study of which, if properly conducted, will enable us more perfectly to read that great book which we call the 'Universe.'" But, over and above this, the Natural Laws will enable us to read that great duplicate which we call the "Unseen Universe," and to think and live in fuller harmony with it. After all, the true greatness of Law lies in its vision of the Unseen. Law in the visible is the Invisible in the visible. And to speak of Laws as Natural is to define them in their application to a part of the universe, the sense-part, whereas a wider survey would lead us to regard all Law as essentially Spiritual. To magnify the Laws of Nature, as Laws of this small world of ours, is to take a provincial view of the universe. Law is great not because the phenomenal world is great, but because these vanishing lines are the avenues into the eternal Order.

"Is it less reverent to regard the universe as an illimitable avenue which leads up to God, than to look upon it as a limited area bounded by an impenetrable wall, which, if we could only pierce it would admit us at once into the presence of the Eternal?" Indeed the authors of the "Unseen Universe" demur even to the expression material universe, since, as they tell us "Matter is (though it may seem paradoxical to say so) the less important half of the material of the physical universe." And even Mr. Huxley, though in a different sense, assures us, with Descartes, "that we know more of mind than we do of body; that the immaterial world is a firmer reality than the material."

How the priority of the Spiritual improves the strength and meaning of the whole argument will be seen at once. The lines of the Spiritual existed first, and it was natural to expect that when the "Intelligence resident in the 'Unseen'" proceeded to frame the material universe He should go upon the lines already laid down. He would, in short, simply project the higher Laws downward, so that the Natural World would become an incarnation, a visible representation, a working model of the spiritual. The whole function of the material world lies here. The world is not a thing that is; it is not. It is a thing that teaches, yet not even a thing—a show that shows, a teaching shadow, However useless the demonstration otherwise, philosophy does well in proving that matter is a non-entity. We work with it as the mathematician with an "x." The reality is alone the Spiritual. "It is very well for physicists to speak of 'matter,' but for men generally to call this 'a material world' is an absurdity. Should we call it an x-world it would mean as much, viz., that we do not know what it is." When shall we learn the true mysticism of one who was yet far from being a mystic—

> "We look not at the things which are seen, but at the things which are not seen; for the things which are seen are temporal, but the things which are not seen are eternal?"

The visible is the ladder up to the invisible; the temporal is but the scaffolding of the eternal. And when the last immaterial souls have climbed through this material to God, the scaffolding shall be taken down, and the earth dissolved with fervent heat—not because it was base, but because its work is done.

"The Watchman at the Gate"

from

The Secret Door to Success (1940)

Florence Scovel Shinn

Florence Scovel Shinn
(1871-1940)

Florence Scovel was born Septemer 24, 1871, in Camden, New Jersey. Her mother was the former Emily Hopkinson of Pennsylvania. Her father was Alden Cortlandt Scovel, and he practiced law in Camden. Besides Florence there was an older daughter and younger son. Florence was educated in Philadelphia at the Friends Central School and studied art at the Pennsylvania Academy of Fine Arts from 1889 to 1897. It was there that she met her future husband, Everett Shinn (1876 - 1953), who was a fairly celebrated painter of impressionistic canvases and realistic murals.

Shortly after Florence's graduation from the Academy, she and Everett were married. The Shinns moved to New York City where they pursued separate careers in art. Everett was interested in the theatre and not only designed and painted for it but built a small theatre in the courtyard behind their studio home at 112 Waverly Place, near Washington Square. He organised the Waverly Players and wrote three plays in each of which Florence played the title role.

Before World War 1 she was an illustrator of popular children's literature in magazines and books. In 1912, after fourteen years of marriage, Everett requested a divorce.

In 1925, having been unable to find a publisher for "The Game of Life and How to Play It" she published it herself. "Your Word is Your Wand" was published in 1928 and "The Secret Door to Success" was published in 1940 shortly before her death on October 17, 1940. The "Power of the Spoken Word" is a compendium of her notes, gathered by a student and published postumously in 1945.

The Watchman at the Gate

"Also I set watchmen over you, saying, Hearken to the sound of the trumpet." –Jeremiah 6:17

We must all have a watchman at the gate of our thoughts. The Watchman at the Gate is the superconscious mind.

We have the power to choose our thoughts.

Since we have lived in the race thought for thousands of years, it seems almost impossible to control them. They rush through our minds like stampeding cattle or sheep.

But a single sheep-dog can control the frightened sheep and guide them into the sheep pen.

I saw a picture in the news-reels of a shepherd dog controlling the sheep. He had rounded up all but three. These three resisted and resented. They baahed and lifted their front feet in protest, but the dog simply sat down in front and never took his eyes off them. He did not bark or threaten. He just sat and looked his determination. In a little while the sheep tossed their heads and went in the pen.

We can learn to control our thoughts in the same way, by gentle determination, not force.

We take an affirmation and repeat it continually, while our thoughts are on the rampage.

We cannot always control our thoughts, but we can control our words, and repetition impresses the subconscious, and we are then master of the situation.

In the sixth chapter of Jeremiah we read: "I set a watchman over you, saying, Hearken to the sound of the trumpet."

Your success and happiness in life depend upon the watchman at the gate of your thoughts, sooner or later, crystallize on the external.

People think by running away from a negative situation, they will be rid of it, but the same situation confronts them wherever they go.

They will meet the same experiences until they have learned their lessons. This idea is brought out in the moving picture, "The Wizard of Oz."

The little girl, Dorothy, is very unhappy because the mean woman in the village wants to take away her dog, Toto. She goes, in despair, to confide in her Aunt Em and Uncle Henry, but they are too busy to listen, and tell her to "run along." She says to Toto, "There is somewhere, a wonderful place high above the skies where everybody is happy and no one is mean." How she would love to be there!

A Kansas cyclone suddenly comes along, and she and Toto are lifted up, high in the sky, and land in the country of Oz. Everything seems very delightful at first, but soon she has the same old experiences. The mean old woman of the village has turned into a terrible witch, and is still trying to get Toto from her.

How she wishes she could be back in Kansas.

She is told to find the Wizard of Oz. He is all powerful and will grant her request. She starts off to find his palace in the Emerald City. On the way she meets a scarecrow. He is so unhappy because he hasn't a brain. She meets a man made of tin, who is so unhappy because he hasn't a heart. Then she meets a lion who is so unhappy because he has no courage. She cheers them up by saying, "We'll all go to the Wizard of Oz and he'll give what we want"—the scarecrow a brain, the tin man a heart, and the lion courage.

They encounter terrible experiences, for the bad witch is determined to capture Dorothy and take away Toto and the ruby slippers which protect her.

At last they reach the Emerald Palace of the Wizard of Oz. They ask for an audience, but are told no one has ever seen the Wizard of Oz, who lives mysteriously in the palace. But through the influence of the good witch of the North, they enter the palace. There they discover the Wizard is just a fake magician from Dorothy's home town in Kansas.

They are all in despair because their wishes cannot be granted!

But then the good witch shows them that their wishes are already granted. The scarecrow has developed a brain by having to decide what to do in the experiences he has encountered, the tin man finds he has a heart because he loves Dorothy, and the lion has become courageous because he had to show courage in his many adventures.

The good witch from the North says to Dorothy, "What have you learned from your experiences?" and Dorothy replies, "I have learned that my heart's desire is in my own home and in my own front yard." So the good witch waves her wand, and Dorothy is at home again.

She wakes up and finds that the scarecrow, the tin man, and the lion are the men who work on her uncle's farm. They are so glad to have her back. This story teaches that if you run away your problems will run after you.

Be undisturbed by a situation, and it will fall away of its own weight.

There is an occult law of indifference. "None of these things move me." "None of these things disturb me" we might say in modern language.

When you can no longer be disturbed, all disturbance will disappear from the external.

"When your eyes have seen your teachers, your teachers disappear."

"I set watchmen over you, saying, Hearken to the sound of the trumpet."

A trumpet is a musical instrument, used in olden times, to draw people's attention to something–to victory, to order.

You will form the habit of giving attention to every thought and word, when you realize their importance.

The imagination, the scissors of the mind, is constantly cutting out the events to come into your life. Many people are cutting out fear-pictures. Seeing things which are not divinely planned.

With the "single eye," man sees only the Truth. He sees through evil, knowing that out of it comes good. He transmutes injustice into justice, and disarms his seeming enemy by sending goodwill.

We read in mythology of the Cyclops, a race of giants, said to have inhabited Sicily. These giants had only one eye in the middle of the forehead. The seat of the imaging faculty is situated in the forehead (between the eyes). So these fabled giants came from this idea.

You are indeed a giant when you have a single eye. Then every thought will be a constructive thought, and every word, a word of Power.

Let the third eye be the watchman at the gate.

"If therefore thine eye be single, thy whole body is full of light."

With the single eye your body will be transformed into your spiritual body, the "body electric" made in God's likeness and image (imagination).

By seeing clearly the perfect plan, we could redeem the world, with our inner eye seeing a world of peace and plenty and goodwill.

"Judge not by appearances, judge righteous judgment."

"Nation shall not lift up sword against nation, neither shall they learn war anymore."

The occult law of indifference means that you are undisturbed by adverse appearances. You hold steadily to the constructive thought, which wins out.

Spiritual law transcends the law of Karma.

This is the attitude of mind which must be held by the healer or practitioner towards his patient.

Indifferent to appearances of lack, loss, or sickness, he brings about the change in mind, body, and affairs.

Let me quote from the thirty-first chapter of Jeremiah. The keynote is one of rejoicing. It gives a picture of the individual freed from negative thinking.

"For there shall be a day that the watchmen upon the mount Ephraim shall cry, Arise ye, and let us go up to Zion unto the Lord our God."

The Watchman at the Gate neither slumbers nor sleeps. It is the "Eye which watches over Israel."

But the individual, living in a world of negative thought is not conscious of this inner eye. He may occasionally have flashes of intuition or illumination, then falls back into a world of chaos.

It takes determination and eternal vigilance to check up on words and thoughts. Thoughts of fear, failure, resentment and ill-will must be dissolved and dissipated.

Take the statement: "Every plant my father in heaven has not planted shall be rooted up."

This gives you a vivid picture of rooting up weeds in a garden. They are thrown aside, and dry up because they are without soil to nourish them.

But the individual, living in a world of negative thought, is not conscious of this inner eye. You nourish negative thoughts by giving them your attention. Use the occult law of indifference and refuse to be interested.

Soon you will starve out the "army of all aliens." Divine ideas will crowd your consciousness, false ideas fade away, and you will desire only that which God desires through you.

The Chinese have a proverb, "The philosopher leaves the cut of his coat to the tailor."

But the individual, living in a world of negative thought, is not conscious of this inner eye.

So leave the plan of your life to the Divine Designer, and you will find all conditions permanently perfect.

> The ground I am on is holy ground. I now expand rapidly into the divine plan of my life, where all conditions are permanently perfect.

Is Disease a Belief?
(1859)

Phineas Parkhurst Quimby

Phineas Parkhurst Quimby
(1802-1866)

Phineas Parkhurst Quimby, who was known as "Park," was born on February 16, 1802, in Lebanon, New Hampshire. Several important elements of his life led to the development of his ideas of mental healing.

The first important milestone was when Quimby developed tuberculosis but became disillusioned with the method of treatment prescribed by his physician and gave up hope of recovery. A friend suggested that he take up a physical outdoor activity such as horseback riding to improve his condition. While his severe physical ailments prevented him from trying this suggestion, Quimby tried the next best thing and embarked on carriage trips. This course of action produced remarkable results and his recovery prompted much thought on the matter. However, he did not pursue this further until several years later.

In 1838, Quimby began studying Mesmerism after attending a lecture by Doctor Collyer and soon began further experimentation with the help of Lucius Burkmar, who could fall into a trance and diagnose illnesses. Quimby again saw the mental and placebo effect of the mind over the body when medicines prescribed by Burkmar, with no physical value, cured patients of diseases. From the conclusions of these studies, Phineas Quimby developed theories of mentally aided healing and opened an office in Portland, Maine in 1859. Among the students and patients who joined his studies and helped him to commit his teachings to writing were Warren Felt Evans, Annetta Seabury Dresser and Julious Dresser, the founders of New Thought as a named movement, and Mary Baker Eddy, the founder of the Christian Science movement.

Dr. Quimby died on Jan. 16, 1866, at his residence in Belfast Maine, where he lived most of his life, at the age of sixty-four years.

Is Disease a Belief?

I say it is, for a person is to himself just what he thinks he is, and he is in his belief sick. If I am sick, I am sick for my feelings are my sickness, and my sickness is my belief, and my belief is my mind; therefore all disease is in the mind or belief. Now as our belief or disease is made up of ideas which are matter, it is necessary to know what ideas we are in; for to cure the disease is to correct the error; and as disease is what follows the error, destroy the cause, and the effect will cease. How can this be done?

By a knowledge of the law of harmony. To illustrate this law of harmony I must take some law that you admit. I will take the law of mathematics. You hear of a mathematical problem. You wish to solve it; the answer is in the problem, the error is in it, the happiness and misery are also in it. Your error is the cause of your sickness or trouble. Now to cure your sickness or trouble is to correct the error. If you knew the real state of things, you would not call on a person who knows no more than you do if you knew the facts.

When I say that all disease is in the mind and that mind is matter, it is to the hearer simply an assertion for he thinks there is no proof of it. All, I suppose, will admit that what we say and believe is attributed to the mind. Again, we say such a person's mind "is disturbed" and "they have lost their mind"; so memory is called mind, and if you forget anything, you say it slipped your mind. Now if I tell you of something you never saw and you believe it, is not your belief mind? Again, is not what a man believes to him knowledge? But should I ask you, if you were ever in London and you say no, yet believe there is such a place or city as London, is not your belief of it, mind, and is not the city in your belief? Now suppose you are standing in one of the parks in London, is that a belief or a fact? If it is a fact, you have no mind about it. Now here you see a city that exists outside of the mind or belief.

Now everything that exists outside of the mind would exist if there was no person to see it, but every person that believes it, to him it exists in a belief. And as a belief is mind, everything that man creates is in the mind and shadowed forth to the mind. For instance, trees exist outside of the mind. When man conceives the idea of making a house, the idea is in the mind, but the timber has no mind. It exists outside, but when the wisdom makes the house, its body represents the idea made in the mind. Now we call the wood of which the house is built matter. Now suppose we think that if we go out-of-doors we shall take cold; the belief is our mind and also the belief that there is something to take or catch. Now this something is like the wood; it is to make something; now all the aforesaid exist in the mind, the same as the wood. The fact that there is something must be a belief for we have not seen it nor felt it any more than we did London, but presently we do feel it; so does it not exist in the feelings or mind? At last we see it and, as we believe, catch it. Now where did it come from? From the cold. Now suppose there never was a person, could that something exist? And if it could not, then it existed in the mind. This shows that the mind is something, call it what you please.

“Thought and Action”

from

Above Life’s Turmoil

James Allen

James Allen
(1864-1912)

James Allen was born in Leicester, Central England on November 28, 1864. The family business failed within a few years, and in 1879 his father left for America in an effort to recoup his losses. The elder Allen had hoped to settle in the United States, but was robbed and murdered before he could send for his family. The financial crisis that resulted forced James to leave school at fifteen. He eventually became a private secretary. He worked in this capacity for several British manufacturers until 1902, when he decided to devote all his time to writing.

Soon after finishing his first book, From Poverty To Power, Allen moved to Ilfracombe, on England's southwest coast. The little resort town with its seafront Victorian hotels and its rolling hills and winding lanes offered him the quiet atmosphere he needed to pursue his philosophical studies.

As A Man Thinketh was Allen's second book. Despite its subsequent popularity he was dissatisfied with it. Even though it was his most concise and eloquent work, the book that best embodied his thought, he somehow failed to recognize its value. His wife Lily had to persuade him to publish it.

Unfortunately, Allen's literary career was short, lasting only nine years, until his death in 1912. During that period he wrote nineteen books, a rich outpouring of ideas that have lived on to inspire later generations.

Thought and Action

As the fruit to the tree and the water to the spring, so is action to thought. It does not come into manifestation suddenly and without a cause. It is the result of a long and silent growth; the end of a hidden process which has long been gathering force. The fruit of the tree and the water gushing from the rock are both the effect of a combination of natural processes in air and earth which have long worked together in secret to produce the phenomenon; and the beautiful acts of enlightenment and the dark deeds of sin are both the ripened effects of trains of thought which have long been harboured in the mind.

The sudden falling, when greatly tempted, into some grievous sin by one who was believed, and who probably believed himself, to stand firm, is seen neither to be a sudden nor a causeless thing when the hidden process of thought which led up to it are revealed. The falling was merely the end, the outworking, the finished result of what commenced in the mind probably years before. The man had allowed a wrong thought to enter his mind; and a second and a third time he had welcomed it, and allowed it to nestle in his heart. Gradually he became accustomed to it, and cherished, and fondled, and tended it; and so it grew, until at last it attained such strength and force that it attracted to itself the opportunity which enabled it to burst forth and ripen into act. As falls the stately building whose foundations have been gradually undermined by the action of water, so at last falls the strong man who allows corrupt thoughts to creep into his mind and secretly undermine his character.

When it is seen that all sin and temptation are the natural outcome of the thoughts of the individual, the way to overcome sin and temptation becomes plain, and its achievement a near possibility, and, sooner or later, a certain reality; for if a man will admit, cherish, and brood upon thoughts that are pure and good, those thoughts, just as surely as the impure, will grow and gather force, and will at last attract to themselves the opportunities which will enable them to ripen into act.

"There is nothing hidden that shall not be revealed," and

every thought that is harboured in the mind must, by virtue of the impelling force which is inherent in the universe, at last blossom into act good or bad according to its nature. The divine Teacher and the sensualist are both the product of their own thoughts, and have become what they are as the result of the seeds of thought which they have implanted, are allowed to fall, into the garden of the heart, and have afterwards watered, tended, and cultivated.

Let no man think he can overcome sin and temptation by wrestling with opportunity; he can only overcome them by purifying his thoughts; and if he will, day by day, in the silence of his soul and in the performance of his duties, strenuously overcome all erroneous inclination, and put in its place thoughts that are true and that will endure the light, opportunity to do evil will give place to opportunity for accomplishing good, for a man can only attract that to him which is in harmony with his nature, and no temptation can gravitate to a man unless there is that in his heart which is capable of responding to it.

Guard well your thoughts, reader, for what you really are in your secret thoughts today, be it good or evil, you will, sooner or later, become in actual deed. He who unwearingly guards the portals of his mind against the intrusion of sinful thoughts, and occupies himself with loving thoughts, with pure, strong, and beautiful thoughts, will, when the season of their ripening comes, bring forth the fruits of gentle and holy deeds, and no temptation that can come against him shall find him unarmed or unprepared.

"Developing New Brain Cells"

from

The Law of Attraction in the Thought World (1906)

William Walker Atkinson

William Walker Atkinson
(1862-1932)

William Walker Atkinson was born in Baltimore, Maryland on December 5, 1862. He married Margaret Foster Black of Beverley, New Jersey on October 1889 and they had two children. He pursued a business career from 1882 onwards and in 1894 he was admitted as an attorney to the Bars of Pennsylvania. Whilst he gained much material success in his profession as a lawyer, the stress and over-strain eventually took its toll, and during this time he experienced a complete physical and mental breakdown, and financial disaster. He looked for healing and in the late 1880's he found it with New Thought.

Some time after his healing, Atkinson began to write some articles on the Truths which he had discovered which was then known as Mental Science, and in 1889 an article by him entitled "A Mental Science Catechism," appeared in Charles Fillmore's new periodical, Modern Thought.

In 1900 he worked as an associate editor of Suggestion, a New Thought journal, and wrote his first book, Thought-Force in Business and Everyday Life, being a series of lessons in personal magnetism, psychic influence, thought-force, concentration, will-power & practical Mental Science.

He then met Sydney Flower, a well-known New Thought publisher and businessman and teamed up with him. In December, 1901 he assumed editorship of Flower's popular New Thought magazine, a post which he held up until 1905.

Atkinson wrote a great many books on New Thought as well, which became very popular and influential among New Thought devotees and practitioners and achieved wide circulation. In 1903, he was admitted to the Bars of Illinois, which means he did not leave that part of his life aside.

William Walker Atkinson died on November 22, 1932, in California–one of the truly greats of The New Thought Movement.

I have spoken of the plan of getting rid of undesirable states of feeling by driving them out. But a far better way is to cultivate the feeling or emotion directly opposed to the one you wish to eradicate.

We are very apt to regard ourselves as the creatures of our emotions and feelings, and to fancy that these feelings and emotions are "we." But such is far from being the truth. It is true that the majority of the race are slaves of their emotions and feelings, and are governed by them to a great degree. They think that feelings are things that rule one and from which one cannot free himself, and so they cease to rebel. They yield to the feeling without question, although they may know that the emotion or mental trait is calculated to injure them, and to bring unhappiness and failure instead of happiness and success. They say, "We are made that way," and let it go at that.

The new Psychology is teaching the people better things. It tells them that they are masters of their emotions and feelings, instead of being their slaves. It tells them that brain-cells may be developed that will manifest along desirable lines, and that the old brain-cells that have been manifesting so unpleasantly may be placed on the retired list, and allowed to atrophy from want of use. People may make themselves over, and change their entire natures. This is not mere idle theory, but is a working fact which has been demonstrated by thousands of people, and which is coming more and more before the attention of the race.

No matter what theory of mind we entertain, we must admit that the brain is the organ and instrument of the mind, in our present state of existence, at least, and that the brain must be considered in this matter. The brain is like a wonderful musical instrument, having millions of keys, upon which we may play innumerable combinations of sounds. We come into the world with certain tendencies, temperaments, and pre-dispositions, We may account for these tendencies by heredity, or we may account for them upon theories of pre-existence, but the facts remain the same. Certain keys seem to respond to our touch more easily than others. Certain notes seem to sound forth as the current of circumstances sweeps over the strings. And certain other notes are less easily vibrated. But we find that if we but make an effort of the will to restrain the utterance of some of these easily sounded strings, they will grow more difficult to sound, and less liable to be stirred by the passing breeze. And if we will pay attention to some of the other strings that have not been giving forth a clear tone, we will soon get them in good working order; their notes will chime forth clear and vibrant, and will drown the less pleasant sounds.

We have millions of unused brain cells awaiting our cultivation. We are using but a few of them, and some of these we are working to death. We are able to give some of these cells a rest, by using other cells. The brain may be trained and cultivated in a manner incredible to one who has not looked into the subject. Mental attitudes may be acquired and cultivated, changed and discarded, at will. There is no longer any excuse for people manifesting unpleasant and harmful mental states. We have the remedy in our own hands.

We acquire habits of thought, feeling, and action, repeated use. We may be born with a tendency in a certain direction, or we may acquire tendencies by suggestions from other; such as the examples of those around us, suggestions from reading, listening to teachers. We are a bundle of mental habits. Each time we indulge in an undesirable thought or habit, the easier does it become for us to repeat that thought or action.

Mental scientists are in the habit of speaking of desirable thoughts or mental attitudes as "positive," and of the undesirable ones as "negative." There is a good reason for this. The mind instinctively recognizes certain things as good for the individual to which it belongs, and it clears the path for such thoughts, and interposes the least resistance to them. They have a much greater effect than an undesirable thought possesses, and one positive thought will counteract a number of negative thoughts. The best way to overcome undesirable or negative thoughts and feelings is to cultivate the positive ones. The positive thought is the strongest plant, and will in time starve out the negative one by withdrawing from it the nourishment necessary for its existence.

Of course the negative thought will set up a vigorous resistance at first, for it is a fight for life with it. In the slang words of the time, it "sees its finish" if the positive thought is allowed to grow and develop; and, consequently it makes things unpleasant for the individual until he has started well into the work of starving it out. Brain cells do not like to be laid on the shelf any more than does any other form of living energy, and they rebel and struggle until they become too weak to do so. The best way is to pay as little attention as possible to these weeds of the mind, but put in as much time as possible watering, caring for and attending to the new and beautiful plants in the garden of the mind.

For instance, if you are apt to hate people, you can best overcome the negative thought by cultivating Love in its place. Think Love, and act it out, as often as possible. Cultivate thoughts of kindness, and act as kindly as you can to everyone with whom you come in contact. You will have trouble at the start, but gradually Love will master Hate, and the latter will begin to droop and wither. If you have a tendency toward the "blues" cultivate a smile, and a cheerful view of things. Insist upon your mouth wearing upturned corners, and make an effort of the will to look upon the bright side of things. The "blue-devils" will set up a fight, of course, but pay no attention to them - just go on cultivating optimism and cheerfulness. Let "Bright, Cheerful and Happy" be your watchword, and try to live it out.

These recipes may seem very old and timeworn, but they are psychological truths and may be used by you to advantage. If you once comprehend the nature of the thing, the affirmations and auto-suggestions of the several schools may be understood and taken advantage of. You may make yourself energetic instead of slothful, active instead of lazy, by this method. It is all a matter of practice and steady work. New Thought people often have much to say about "holding the thought;" and, indeed, it is necessary to "hold the thought" in order to accomplish results. But something more is needed. You must "act out" the thought until it becomes a fixed habit with you. Thoughts take form in action; and in turn actions influence thought. So by "acting out" certain lines of thought, the actions react upon the mind, and increase the development of the part of the mind having close relation to the act. Each time the mind entertains a thought, the easier becomes the resulting action - and each time an act is performed, the easier becomes the corresponding thought. So you see the thing works both ways - action and reaction. If you feel cheerful and happy, it is very natural for you to laugh. And if you will laugh a little, you will begin to feel bright and cheerful. Do you see what I am trying to get at? Here it is, in a nutshell: if you wish to cultivate a certain habit of action, begin by cultivating the mental attitude corresponding to it. And as a means of cultivating that mental attitude, start in to "act out" or go through, the motions of the act corresponding to the thought. Now, see if you cannot apply this rule. Take up something that you really feel should be done, but which you do not feel like doing. Cultivate the thought leading up to it. Say to yourself: "I like to do so and so," and then go through the motions (cheerfully, remember!) and act out the thought that you like to do the thing. Take an interest in the doing—study out the best way to do it—put brains into it—take a pride in it—and you will find yourself doing the thing with a considerable amount of pleasure and interest. You will have cultivated a new habit.

If you prefer trying it on some mental trait of which you wish to be rid, it will work the same way. Start in to cultivate the opposite trait, and think it out and act it out for all you are worth. Then watch the change that will come over you. Don't be discouraged at the resistance you will encounter at first, but sing gaily: "I can and I will," and get to work in earnest. The important thing in this work is to keep cheerful and interested. If you manage to do this, the rest will be easy.

Images of Original Material

Charles F. Haanel

The Master-Key System

THE MASTER KEY SYSTEM

707-709-711 PINE STREET
SAINT LOUIS, MISSOURI

Letter of Transmittal, Part Two.

Dear Friend:

Our difficulties are largely due to confused ideas and ignorance of our true interests. The great task is to discover the laws of nature to which we are to adjust ourselves. Clear thinking and moral insight are, therefore, of incalculable value. All processes, even those of thought, rest on solid foundations.

The keener the sensibilities, the more acute the judgment, the more delicate the taste, the more refined the moral feelings, the more subtile the intelligence, the loftier the aspiration - the purer and more intense are the gratifications which existence yields. Hence it is that the study of the best that has been thought in the world gives supreme pleasure.

The powers, uses and possibilities of the mind under new interpretations are incomparably more wonderful than the most extravagant accomplishment, or even dreams of material progress. Thought is energy. Active thought is active energy; concentrated thought is concentrated energy. Thought concentrated on a definite purpose becomes power. This is the power which is being used by those who do not believe in the virtue of poverty, or the beauty of self-denial. They perceive that this is the talk of weaklings.

The ability to receive and manifest this power depends upon the ability to recognize the Infinite Energy ever dwelling in man, constantly creating and recreating his body and mind, and ready at any moment to manifest through him in any needful manner. In exact proportion to the recognition of this truth will be the manifestation in the outer life of the individual.

Part two explains the method by which this is accomplished.

Yours sincerely,

Charles F. Haanel

An installment of The Master Key System as originally mailed to students of the course. Circa 1917.

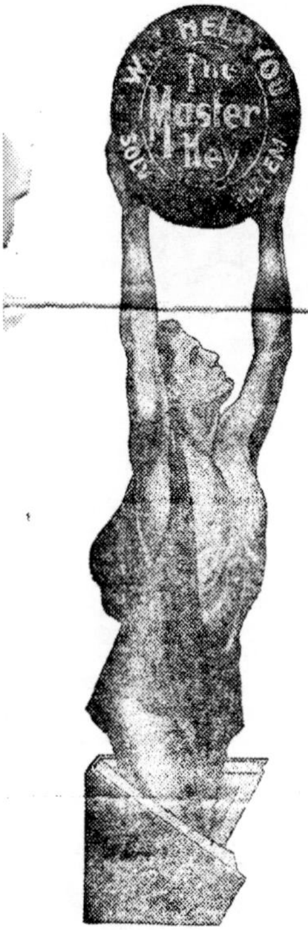

REG. U. S. PAT. OFF.

General Instructions to Students

1. The Master Key System is copyrighted, and can not properly be copied, loaned or made the basis of sale, barter or exchange.

2. The Master Key System consists of twenty-four parts, names of students are placed on an addressing machine and one part is mailed each week. They go forward automatically, and cannot be sent more frequently nor can they be held back.

3. All parts should be kept together where they can be quickly and readily referred to at any time.

4. Read the first part at least once each day until the second part comes. Then write the replies to the questions in the first part, cut off and mail to me.

5. Read the second part each day until the third part comes, answer the questions and continue in like manner until you have finished the course.

6. The papers will be returned to you with the correct replies for comparison. See how many questions were answered exactly right, how many were nearly right. See where you entirely failed to get the thought which was intended.

7. Practice the exercises for concentration and visualization until you are certain that you have secured perfect control of your thought processes.

8. If you do not readily grasp the thought in any part, the next part will probably make it clear.

9. Make a personal application of every method suggested, apply it in your daily experience.

10. Write letters concerning personal problems, or asking questions, on a separate sheet of paper.

11. If a part comes before you are ready for it, put it aside until you are ready. There is no occasion for haste.

12. Any error or omission will be promptly adjusted, but in this case, write, do not return the paper.

13. Use a good quality of black ink or a typewriter.

14. Write your name and FULL address on each sheet or letter.

15. Remember there are twenty-four parts, and that each part is necessary for a complete understanding of the subject, the Master-Key System is therefore never sold except as a complete work; parts are never sold separately.

16. Report any omission or error promptly. The Master-Key service is intended to be as nearly perfect as possible, and your co-operation, looking to this end will be much appreciated.

17. The letters of transmittal which reach you weekly should be carefully preserved with the lesson with which they are sent. The letter always contains a thought of particular value in connection with the lesson. They are of much value in your study.

Bound Volume

18. The bound volume is never sold to any one at any price, unless they have completed the study and made payment in full.

The Fellowship Department will assist in the solution of any problem. Thousands of students are finding the solution to every conceivable problem through the help received from this source.

Diplomas Students who complete the course and who hold a receipt in full for all payments, will be entitled to receive a diploma.

Trade Mark Notice The words "the Master Key" and the figure holding the emblem are both registered in the United States patent offices and in Great Britain and other foreign countries as a trade mark, and all rights therein are reserved and will be protected.

The "General Instructions to Students" include instructions to do the exercises, make practical applications, that the bound volume is only available to those who complete the course, and that students who complete the course will be entitled to a diploma.

PART TWO

Reply to the following questions, cut off and mail to me.

11. What are the two modes of mental activity?

12. Upon what do ease and perfection depend?

13. What is the value of the sub-conscious?

14. What are some of the functions of the conscious mind?

15 How has the distinction between the conscious and the sub-conscious been expressed?

16. What method is necessary in order to impress the sub-conscious?

17. What will be the result?

18. What is the result of the operation of this law?

19. What name has been given to this law?

20. How is this law stated?

Name............................ Address...... ....

City............................State................ ....

NOTE

Upon receipt of your replies to these questions, a sheet containing the correct reply to each question will be sent to you This will not only be interesting for comparison, but will be an invaluable source of reference.

The Questions and Answers section in an original installment of The Master Key System course. The note at the bottom states "Upon receipt of your replies to these questions, a sheet containing the correct reply to each question will be sent to you."

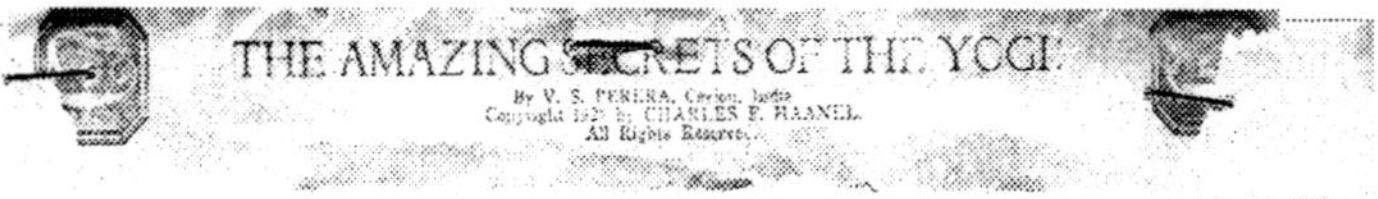

LETTER OF TRANSMITTAL.

Dear Friend:-

In accordance with your request, the first lesson in Yoga Philosophy is enclosed herewith.

As you progress with your study of this philosophy, you will find that much which heretofore seemed incomprehensible will become perfectly clear.

You will discover that you possess remarkable powers, which perhaps you may not heretofore have used to advantage.

You will break through the fictitious walls of limitation, for no matter how successful we may be, there always seems to be limitation somewhere.

Your social, business and financial affairs will take on new life, you will become familiar with the laws of Mastery and Leadership.

In fact you will find the study a "Great Adventure", which will enable you to handle every situation which may confront you, in the best possible manner.

Remember that every desire has its means of accomplishment, every question has its answer, and somewhere in these unusual, remarkable lessons the thought will come to you, which will enable you to scale the heights, to realize the dreams which sometimes seemed unattainable.

These lessons do not consist of beautiful theories, they consist of concrete methods which have been demonstrated over and over again for centuries, but which have heretofore been given only by word of mouth, and to those only who have been considered prepared to receive them.

It will be your privilege to be associated with a great body of enthusiastic and magnetic personalities whose influence will do much to render your environment congenial and harmonious for it is well known that we gravitate toward the things with which we become associated.

A diploma suitable for framing is yours if the replies to questions show that you are entitled to it.

Trusting that the good things of life may come to you in unfailing abundance, I remain,

Yours sincerely,

Charles F. Haanel

The Letter of Transmittal from the original course for "The Amazing Secrets of the Yogi." The second to last paragraph reads, "A diploma suitable for framing is yours if the replies to questions show that you are entitled to it." Circa 1929.

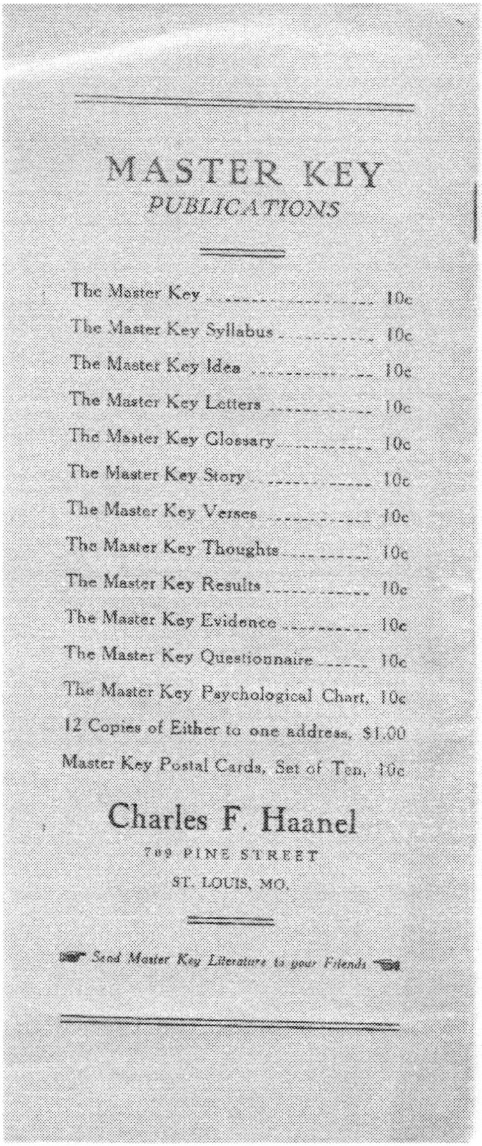

MASTER KEY
PUBLICATIONS

The Master Key	10c
The Master Key Syllabus	10c
The Master Key Idea	10c
The Master Key Letters	10c
The Master Key Glossary	10c
The Master Key Story	10c
The Master Key Verses	10c
The Master Key Thoughts	10c
The Master Key Results	10c
The Master Key Evidence	10c
The Master Key Questionnaire	10c
The Master Key Psychological Chart,	10c
12 Copies of Either to one address,	$1.00
Master Key Postal Cards, Set of Ten,	10c

Charles F. Haanel
709 PINE STREET
ST. LOUIS, MO.

Send Master Key Literature to your Friends

From The Master Key Psychological Chart brochure, this is the back cover. It lists the publications that Charles F. Haanel had available, including "The Master Key Lessons", "The Master Key Verses", and "The Master Key Evidence". All were ten cents apiece.

If

Rudyard Kipling

Rudyard Kipling
(1865-1936)

Rudyard Kipling was born in Bombay in 1865. His father was John Lockwood Kipling and his mother, Alice, was the sister of Lady Burne-Jones.

In 1871 Kipling was brought home from India and spent five unhappy years with a foster family in Southsea. It was during his time at the college that he began writing poetry and "Schoolboy Lyrics" was published privately in 1881. In the following year he started work as a journalist in India, and while there, produced a body of work, stories, sketches and poems, notably "Plain Tales from the Hills" (1888), which made him an instant literary celebrity.

In 1892 he married an American, Caroline Balestier, and from 1892 to 1896 they lived in Vermont, where Kipling wrote "The Jungle Book," published in 1894. In 1901 came "Kim" and in 1902 the "Just So Stories."

From 1902 Kipling made his home in Sussex, but he continued to travel widely. The stories he subsequently wrote, "A Diversity of Creatures" (1917), "Debits and Credits" (1926), and "Limits and Renewals" (1932) are now thought by many to contain some of his finest writing. The death of his only son in 1915 also contributed to a new inwardness of vision.

Kipling refused to accept the role of Poet Laureate and other civil honours, but he was the first English writer to be awarded the Nobel Prize, in 1907. He died in 1936.

If you can keep your head when all about you
Are losing theirs and blaming it on you;
If you can trust yourself when all men doubt you,
But make allowance for their doubting too:
If you can wait and not be tired by waiting,
Or, being lied about, don't deal in lies,
Or being hated don't give way to hating,
And yet don't look too good, nor talk too wise;

If you can dream—and not make dreams your master;
If you can think—and not make thoughts your aim,
If you can meet with Triumph and Disaster
And treat those two impostors just the same:.
If you can bear to hear the truth you've spoken
Twisted by knaves to make a trap for fools,
Or watch the things you gave your life to, broken,
And stoop and build'em up with worn-out tools;

If you can make one heap of all your winnings
And risk it on one turn of pitch-and-toss,
And lose, and start again at your beginnings,
And never breathe a word about your loss:
If you can force your heart and nerve and sinew
To serve your turn long after they are gone,
And so hold on when there is nothing in you
Except the Will which says to them: "Hold on!"

If you can talk with crowds and keep your virtue,
Or walk with Kings—nor lose the common touch,
If neither foes nor loving friends can hurt you,
If all men count with you, but none too much:
If you can fill the unforgiving minute
With sixty seconds' worth of distance run,
Yours is the Earth and everything that's in it,
And—which is more—you'll be a Man, my son!

Other titles from Kallisti Publishing...

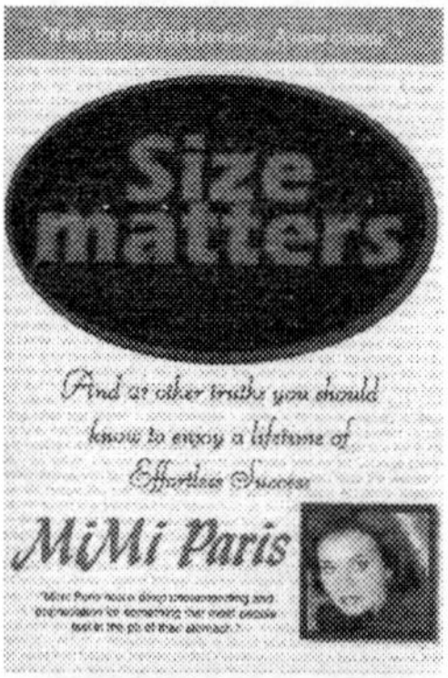

Size Matters!

Mimi Paris

We use untruths to make ourselves feel okay with how we navigate our way through life. These untruths actually keep us from living the life we really want. By learning the truth and living the truth, you will attract success effortlessly and enjoy abundance financially and socially. So, let's tell the truth: Size matters!

Getting Connected Through Exceptional Leadership

Karl Walinskas

Management does not equate leadership. This handbook will show you in simple ways how to transcend stale, ordinary management practices and master the art of connecting with others through extraordinary leadership skill. Take control of your life as a leader–get this book now!

Road Map for National Security: Imperative for Change

U.S. Commission on National Security

Within this report is a plan to strengthen America from the inside, including suggestions on everything from recapitalizing on America's strengths in science and education. This book could not have come at a better time! It's a must read.

www.kallistipublishing.com

www.thefreemasterkey.com

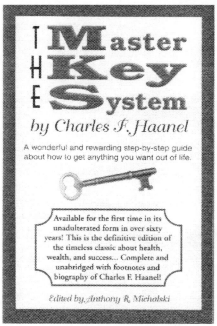

If you enjoyed this book,
then you'll love
The Complete Master Key Course!

www.thecompletemasterkeycourse.com